SERENDIPITY

Chance Pilgrimages

Anne Greco

Praise for *Serendipity*

"Reading these pilgrimage stories was a tonic for my soul. Ms. Greco has got a knack for telling her own tales of pilgrimage in such a way that it will help you recognize your own. If you've ever gotten down on your knees and asked for help this book is a catalog of prayers, like yours, being answered. The miraculous stories are poignantly (and often irreverently) told yet leave me fully inspired and excited to read whatever Ms. Greco writes next. For anyone who has ever had spirit call them to the most unexpected places...this book fairly shouts, "Go!! Go!" You will be glad you did."

Sarah Bamford Seidelmann, author of
Swimming with Elephants, Born to Freak, and
What the Walrus Knows

"Stories give form, color and shape to experience. They are the heart's way of weaving, one thread at a time, a coherent narrative - a life of meaning. In this thoroughly readable collection of personal pilgrimage stories, Anne Greco weaves together the threads of her lifetime conversation with the divine through the souvenirs she's collected along the way. In her beautiful stories, a shell rediscovered at the bottom of a handbag, a photo taken with a rock star, a heart shaped stone - trace the thread of memory - sacred and profane - around the world, back to the heart."

Amy Oscar, author of *Sea of Miracles: An Invitation from the Angels*

"Anne Greco takes us on an intimate pilgrimage of self. It is a powerful reminder of the importance of embracing the energy around us so that we can live life to the fullest, no matter what direction it may lead us."

Jennifer Criswell, author of *At Least You're in Tuscany*

No part of this publication may be reproduced, distributed, or transmitted in any form or by any means, including photocopying, recording, or other electronic or mechanical methods, without the prior written permission of the author except in the case of brief quotations embodied in critical reviews and certain other non-commercial uses permitted by copyright law. For permission requests, write to the publisher at annegrecowriter.com.

© 2017 Anne Greco
All rights reserved.

ISBN: 0692903607
ISBN 13: 9780692903605

*This book is lovingly dedicated to
Alanna Kali and Emily Rose, Annette and Joe,
and Martin.*

This discovery indeed is almost of that kind which I call Serendipity, a very expressive word, which I shall endeavor to explain to you...I once read a silly fairy tale called "The Three Princes of Serendip:" as their highnesses traveled they were always making discoveries, by accidents and sagacity, of things they were not in quest of...

Horace Walpole in a letter to his friend, Horace Mann, 1754

FORWARD

I believe that there is a force larger than us, a force from which everything and everyone emanates and a spark of which we all carry within us. As I wrote on pilgrimage, I found myself using references to this Higher Power interchangeably. Sometimes I'd write of God, other times I'd refer to the Divine or the Universe. The multiple references are not meant to confuse or disrespect; there just isn't one term that I use consistently. Early one morning (3:00 a.m., to be precise) when I was pondering on whether I had to be consistent in my terminology, I received a "wink" in response. I often think of this force as Abundant Love, and so came the answer.

"You can call me A.L.," was the response.

I loved the humor and playfulness that came in the answer–A.L. for Abundant Love. While I don't use the term A.L. in this book, it's how I'm increasingly referring to God. A.L. is joyful, loving, giving, and omnipresent. I like walking with A.L.

INTRODUCTION
THE SHELL

The geographical pilgrimage is the symbolic acting out of an internal journey. One can have one without the other. It is best to have both.

Thomas Merton

I plopped down on the Ethan Allen hand-me-down sofa and reached for my purse. In the search for my car keys I began tossing out Kleenex, business cards, three pens, Altoids, a hairbrush, lipstick, old shopping lists, a wallet, and a small journal. I unzipped the rarely used side pockets. In the first one,

I reverently removed (rather than tossed) a small wooden rosary, laminated holy cards for various saints, and a dog-eared index card that held my daily affirmation.

Still keyless, I opened the other side pocket. There, at the bottom, my fingers wrapped around an unexpected object - a small, dark scallop shell. I didn't remember putting it there. Had it come from the trip to the beach a few weeks ago? My daughters, Alanna and Emily, now young adults, were with me at the shore that weekend, but they were well past the age of putting things in my purse for safekeeping. The shell was not so spectacular as to cause me to purposely pick it out of the sand and carry among the shifting pile of beach chairs, towels, and books back to the beach house. Why did I have it?

"Anne, do you have the keys?"

My husband, Martin's, question jolted me back to reality – and the key search.

"No," I responded, turning the shell over in my hand.

"What's that?"

"A shell; it was in my purse. You didn't put it there the last time we were at the beach, did you?"

"No. Why would I do that?"

"I don't know. It's weird."

Weird is a description that often comes up when synchronicities appear in my life. And this *weird* didn't disappoint. Having no luck finding the keys by the normal means of overturning the house, I did what any girl raised Catholic would do; I prayed to Saint Anthony, patron saint of lost objects.

Saint Anthony, Saint Anthony, please come around. Something is lost and it must be found.

"I found the keys, Anne," Martin shouted from the kitchen. "You left them on the counter."

As always, Saint Anthony had come through.

The errand we had intended to run was no longer important. I was distracted by the shell. I couldn't put it down, staring at it as if it were some object foreign to my world, like, say, a moon rock. I turned it over in my hand, tracing its fan shape. As I placed it on the table, part of a Sir Walter Raleigh poem I'd read in college suddenly came to mind.

Give me my scallop shell of quiet,
My staff of faith to walk upon,
My scrip of joy, immortal diet,
My bottle of salvation,
My gown of glory, hope's true gage,
And thus I'll take my pilgrimage.

The poem was called *His Pilgrimage*. Like falling dominoes, the poem triggered a remembrance of Chaucer's *The Canterbury Tales* (I was an English major in college) which centered on a pilgrimage to Canterbury Cathedral. And from Canterbury my mind jumped to Spain and *the* connection with the shell. The scallop shell was the badge of the pilgrimage to Santiago de Compostela, the burial place of Saint James, the fisherman; its image still marking this pilgrimage route called El Camino de Santiago or the Way of Saint James.

My living room was suddenly filled with ghosts of medieval wanderers, earth-colored clothes, walking sticks in hand, ready to step onto the dusty road that would lead them to their place of religious fulfillment. Pilgrimages: the word hadn't come to mind in years and then it was referred to in a secular way. "Oh, it's much smaller than you might have imagined. But I guess at the time it was quite a mansion," said a friend as she recounted her pilgrimage to Graceland, Elvis Presley's home in Memphis. Acquaintances in my yoga class had spoken about traveling to Arizona for a nature-based pilgrimage to experience the power of Sedona's red rocks.

Growing up Catholic, though, I first associated pilgrimage with travel of a religious purpose. The word conjured up images of people journeying a long distance from home, alone or with a group, navigating difficult terrain to seek redemption, petition for a favor, or give thanks, encountering countless

Serendipity

challenges (physical and spiritual) along the way. Pilgrims continue to walk the Camino, taking upwards of six weeks to complete the 500-mile route. Some also still make the pilgrimage from London to Canterbury Cathedral like those pilgrims in Chaucer's tale.

I began attending Catholic elementary school in the early 1960s at the ripe old age of four. Each night from first grade on I was drilled in Catechism by stock questions and rote answers.

"Who is God?" my mother would ask me as we sat at the pink, Formica-topped kitchen table under the glare of the overhead light.

"God is the Supreme Bean who made heaven and earth," I recited night after night, my young mind conjuring up an image of a large kidney bean. My mother, obviously not listening, never corrected me. *So this is God*, I'd think, made all the more confusing whenever I watched my mother make pasta e fagioli, adding beans to the soup pot. My mistake was eventually corrected in second grade when I received a pocket-sized illustrated child's prayer book for my First Holy Communion. The gold-rimmed pictures showed me that God was not a bean after all; he looked like a bearded old man. He was less intimidating as a bean, though.

At the mature age of six, I made the decision to become a nun when I grew up. Blame it on the movie

The Sound of Music, which I play-acted every day after school. I was praised by our teaching nuns as being an example of a good Catholic girl for considering a religious vocation. One day, Sister Louis Joseph called me to the front of my first-grade classroom. I obediently rose from my chair, straightened my navy blue uniform, and pulled up my sagging knee socks. Thirty-nine heads turned to look at me (yes, there were 40 students in the class). I began the long walk down the narrow aisle between the rows of desks, my legs getting heavier as I approached the blackboard and Sister.

I stopped at her feet. My eyes began traveling up her floor-length blue habit which was covered with a blue sleeveless apron. My eyes moved up to the long, wooden rosary that encircled her waist and then to the large silver crucifix that hung from a chain around her neck. They traveled up to the stiff white wimple that covered shoulders and neck. Her head was wrapped in white cotton so that only her stern face showed. No ears, no hair – this woman did not seem human. A black, waist-length veil capped her habit. Our eyes met. I was so scared that I briefly forgot to breathe.

"Class, Anne is considering entering the convent when she becomes an adult," Sister Louis Joseph announced as she spun me around to face my classmates. "This is truly commendable."

Serendipity

What had possessed me to reveal that secret to Sister on the playground at recess? I felt too guilty now to tell her that my calling had less to do with religious vocation than it had to do with the huge crush I had on Christopher Plummer as Captain von Trapp. Walking back to my desk, my eyes remained glued to the holy card that I clutched in my hands; my reward now coveted by the other children. I avoided their stares as well as those of the large, intimidating statues of the saints who shared our classroom space.

We learned to identify the saints by their iconography, items that were usually associated with their martyrdom. Saint Lucy, patron saint of the blind, stood before us holding her eyeballs which had been gouged out, on a plate. Saint Sebastian's body was pierced by arrows. I may have had a misguided belief that I was going to become a nun, but I never aspired to become a saint. It looked too painful. We listened wide-eyed as the nuns regaled us with stories of saints such as Francis of Assisi (not as scary as Lucy and Sebastian; he was probably the first dog whisperer on record). Years later, I would hear of our parish sponsoring trips to Italy called pilgrimages, with the express purpose of visiting the towns where these saints had lived and died. I was intrigued. An Alitalia flight to Italy, though, didn't seem as challenging as the dangerous routes that medieval pilgrims had to navigate.

Canterbury Tales

Whanne that Aprille with his shoures soute
The droghte of Marche hath perced to the roote.
                    Prologue, *The Canterbury Tales*

I was re-introduced to the idea of pilgrimage in high school when forced to read Chaucer's *The Canterbury Tales*, one of the greatest works of literature, in which twenty-nine pilgrims and a narrator travel to the shrine of the martyred Saint Thomas Beckett at Canterbury Cathedral. During the walk from London to Canterbury and back the pilgrims entertained each other with stories in a competition to win a prize for the best tale.

I didn't understand what I was reading, and didn't for a moment believe the teacher's overview when he said that it was written in English. I use the term reading in a broad sense as we were made to try to decipher the text in its original 14th-century Middle English. Shifting between the original and its modern English translation made my head spin. I just wanted to get through the stories told by the pilgrims to be able to pass the test. Lost on me at the time were the social and religious commentaries embedded in the tales. Hell, I even missed the naughty bits, proof positive that good literature, like youth, is wasted on the young. But I remember feeling a ping of resonance when I again heard the word *pilgrimage*.

Serendipity

Pilgrimages cut across all religions as acts related to devotion, thanksgiving, or penance.

Catholics often make pilgrimages to view and venerate relics, most often the remains of a saint. While the authenticity of the relics may be challenged, pilgrims remain undeterred. Such skepticism is not new. From the time of Chaucer (roughly 800 years ago), cottage industries grew around the sale of "relics" to pilgrims. Pardoners, like the one mentioned in *The Canterbury Tales*, were employed by the Catholic Church during the Middle Ages to sell indulgences to reduce the amount of time a sinner would have to spend in purgatory after death. The deceptive Pardoner in *The Canterbury Tales* sold pig bones as relics to the unsuspecting.

A few years ago, a family friend visited the shrine of Saint Katherine Drexel and bought me a third-degree relic, a tiny piece of white cloth pressed into a laminated holy card. I had no idea that relics had levels. As it was explained to me, first-degree relics are the actual physical remains of the saint. Second-degree relics are items like clothing which were touched by the saint while alive. Third-degree relics, like my piece of cotton fabric, are items that were touched to a first- or second-degree relic. This was starting to sound like some religious form of "six degrees of separation."

Medieval pilgrims purchased badges that were most some of the earliest mass-produced souvenirs.

Stamped metal images of the pilgrimage site or of the venerated saint, these badges were worn as a symbol of the pilgrimage. They were also believed to possess the power to provide the wearer with the protection of the saint to whom the pilgrimage was made. And let's not forget about money. The badges were also of commercial value, providing income to both the pilgrimage site and the local tradesmen who produced the items. Gift shops filled with postcards and tea towels came later, I guess.

"Anne, what are you doing? Are we running those errands? Because if we aren't then I'm going to mow the lawn." I could hear the exasperation in Martin's voice.

"Oh, sorry. No, we don't need to go out now. Mow the lawn. This shell has me thinking."

"The shell has you thinking? About what? It's just a shell."

"No, Martin, it's more than a shell. It was in my purse for a reason."

"Okay. I'll play along. What's the reason?" Martin, my second husband, was indulging me. He had learned through our courtship that I believed that coincidences and synchronicities were messages, signs, and evidence of Divine guidance.

"I was thinking about pilgrimages that I've taken and how they have changed me."

"What pilgrimages have you taken? I never heard you speak about pilgrimages. And what in

Serendipity

the world would make you think of pilgrimages this morning?"

I explained to Martin the symbol of the shell. While the shell had initially started an internal conversation in the broad sense about pilgrimages, it soon became a catalyst for remembering my own pilgrimages. Some of these pilgrimages were intended, some were happenstance, some were religious, some were nature-based, some were secular, and one did not involve any physical travel at all. For some I crossed the Atlantic Ocean, for another I only crossed a local river, and for one I traveled no further than my yoga mat. These pilgrimages took me to places that realigned me with my true self, my soul. At each pilgrimage site I felt as if I gathered a tiny bit of myself that had somehow scattered.

The pilgrimage sites spoke to me in a language that I initially didn't understand but one that turned out to really be my native language. It was a language that I had somehow forgotten and was remembering: that of unconditional love spoken by the Divine. The pilgrimages reminded me in soft whispers and gentle pulls that the Divine resides within me. This revelation was not dramatic; I wasn't struck by a thunderbolt of awareness or transfixed by a heavenly shaft of light as an incoming message from God. Rather, it was subtle, very subtle. Softness enveloped me at each site, creating a peace that reached deep within. My physical senses were heightened at these sites. I heard more, I saw more. I listened to my intuition. I went where I was directed. I stopped and spoke with people to whom I was guided. I participated in activities to which I was led. In doing so, my physical and spiritual boundaries expanded. The pilgrimages cracked me open to reveal the beautiful gem called my soul that resided within.

Early in my first marriage my husband and I lived in Boulder, Colorado. Eventually we moved back to the East Coast where our daughters, Alanna and Emily, were born. We returned to Colorado with the girls for a vacation when they were young. They loved panning for gold in the cold mountain streams surrounding Estes Park. They'd kick off their sandals and tentatively step into the stream, dipping their little sifting pans into the clear, rushing water. Nothing. To ease their disappointment in not striking it rich I took them to a store on the main street that sold rocks and minerals. They were immediately drawn to the large rose quartz stones on a table.

"Girls, come over here," I said, nodding to a pile of very plain looking rocks.

Alanna ran up to the table first. "Mom, we don't want one of those ugly rocks. Can we please pick one of the pretty rocks? Maybe a sparkly purple one?"

"Nope. Pick one of these geodes."

Reluctantly, their tiny hands each picked a geode out of the pile.

Serendipity

"Now, take them to that man standing behind the counter."

The girls obligingly handed their geodes to the clerk. "Now watch girls," the man directed as he tapped a small hammer against the rock. After a few strikes, the dull geode cracked open to reveal an internal cavity that was lined with sparkling crystals just waiting for the light to expose its beauty. The girls' eyes widened. "Mommy, this is magic. They are bee-you-ti-ful," exclaimed Emily drawing out the syllables. I felt like something similar was done to me through the pilgrimages, as if the Divine tapped me open to reveal to me my inner beauty.

I also noticed that my thoughts were less constricted when I was at the pilgrimage sites. I opened my arms and my heart to receive, which was not always easy or natural for me. I loosened my grip on the need to control everything in my life. At each site I gave my problems and petitions over to God, sometimes alone in wordless prayer, sometimes in unison with a group. Faith bubbled up as an innate knowing that I was being heard and that I would be provided for, releasing the need to know the particulars.

Not all of the pilgrimages were intentional but I now understand that I was called to each site at a time when my soul was hungry and in need of nourishment. Serendipity. Sometimes I experience a call to what my physical body needs through food cravings, like, for an example, an insatiable desire for lemons or cranberries. When I do the research as to what vitamins these craved foods provide I realize that my body was shouting out for these specific nutrients. I listen to my body and I give it what it tells me it needs – while being a bit discriminating. Dark chocolate bars infused with sea salt tend to raise a red flag. In hindsight I see that through the pilgrimages my soul was pulling me to what was needed for healing and growth. My journeys began in the most mundane ways. They might have been sparked by hearing a simple word or phrase or a song on the radio, by a phone call or a book recommendation.

While seemingly disparate these pilgrimages shared common elements. Each included some form of a journey. Although not always physical, the journeys were always spiritual and transformational. With each I experienced some form of ecstasy, meaning an expanded spiritual awareness, an encounter with the Divine. (I don't mean to conjure up images of ecstasy as seen in Saint Teresa of Avila's encounter with the angel. But if you visit Rome, I highly recommend seeking out the tiny church, Santa Maria della Vittoria, to experience Bernini's sublime sculpture, *The Ecstasy of Saint Teresa.*) Each pilgrimage asked me to step fully into my life. And finally, with all these pilgrimages, I returned home transformed, renewed, and humbled. Well, okay, I also brought home

Serendipity

souvenirs as mementos of each site to which I traveled, which usually included at least one tea towel. I invite you to return with me through these pages to my pilgrimage sites. Like the travelers in Chaucer's tales, I'll keep you entertained as we go along. It's my hope that you'll begin to recall your own pilgrimages or be inspired to make a pilgrimage of your own.

CHAPTER 1
ASK THE ANGELS

Ask the angels who they're calling,
Go ask the angels if they're calling to thee.

Patti Smith

"Anne, I finally got you!"

I could hear the relief in my friend's voice as only teenage girls can dramatize. It was January 1977. A newly minted 18-year-old, I was standing in the pink kitchen of my parents' home, holding the avocado-green wall phone with the six-foot cord. I had just walked in the front door.

"Do you know who's coming to the Mike Douglas Show tomorrow? Patti!" she blurted, not pausing for me to answer. I didn't need a last name. I knew she was talking about Patti Smith, later termed the Godmother of Punk. As I had closed out my high-school days the year before, I had become obsessed with Patti Smith. I emulated her; she was strong, fearless, and spoke her mind. Plus, she was dead cool.

I was introduced to her music in Home Economics class in between making biscuits and strawberry shortcake. There were eight kitchenettes in the classroom, and my kitchen mate happened to be the only boy in the class. Joe was there not so much to learn as to eat. He was into punk rock, avant-garde at the time. We spent our time measuring ingredients while talking about the music of Tom Verlaine and Television, the Ramones, Richard Hell, Iggy Pop, and Patti Smith-all unknown at the time to most of the record-buying teen population. I fell for Joe quick and hard, first listening to Patti Smith to have something to talk to him about. But Joe quickly grew less important to me than Patti.

Patti Smith and I both had South Jersey roots. She had escaped its confines with grit, determination and, most importantly, an unfailing belief in herself. Strong, confident, and self-assured, she quickly became my role model. I changed my wardrobe to mimic hers; she wore ballet shoes so I bought

Serendipity

pink ones and dyed them black. They weren't soled for outdoor use, but what the fuck. Oh yeah, I had begun to speak like Patti, too.

I lived with my family in a split-level house built in 1969. The décor, in true Italian-American style, was a bit nontraditional, at least compared to the Colonial-style furniture that graced the homes of my non-Italian friends. I think my mother was still under the influence of the Summer of Love when she decorated her new home; she chose a pretty groovy color scheme. An orange wallpapered hall led to my bedroom. The trim on my outer door was painted orange with what I swear was a uranium-based paint. It was the same orange color as that early Fiestaware pottery that was a tad radioactive. A large, orange-colored pleather seat encircled the wooden support beam in the middle of the family room. Two orange chairs and two yellow chairs flanked the stone fireplace. An oil painting on black velvet of Hoboken-born Frank Sinatra, the patron saint of New Jersey, hung on a paneled wall. The stereo was behind the wet bar. This was the only place where I could play *Horses,* Patti Smith's debut album. There was no playing that stereo quietly; the speakers were large enough to be pieces of furniture. So, Patti's voice traveling up the grey-carpeted staircase, around the plastic trees that "grew" in stone planters along the foyer wall, and up to the kitchen where my mother usually sat in the evening after dinner.

"What is that braying I hear?" she would shout down to me. "Lower that." I'd grudgingly oblige while continuing to study the album cover. Patti, dressed in a white man's shirt with torn cuffs, black jacket slung over her shoulder (a bit reminiscent of Sinatra's poses, come to think of it), a horse pin on the jacket's lapel. She had a come hither look – beckoning me in a nonsexual way to join her, to leave South Jersey, free myself of its confines, open up, and branch out.

Down in Vineland, there's a clubhouse. My girlfriend and I spent our weekends visiting Patti's South Jersey stomping grounds, driving through the places that she wrote about, the neighborhoods where she had lived, worked, and attended school. Map unfolded between us, we'd plot the next adventure – Vineland, Woodbury, Mantua, Pitman, Deptford – we hit them all. The old, rusty car lacked heat, which made for less than pleasant rides in the winter. Undeterred, we'd drape a blanket over our laps, reposition the map, scrape the ice off the inside of the windshield and drive into the most rural parts of South Jersey. The landscape, dotted with pig farms and abandoned factories, rendered bucolic musings an impossibility. But there was tenacity to the land and the people- a 1970s version of *The Grapes of Wrath*-hardscrabble and gritty.

Serendipity

I wrote my high school senior thesis on Patti. I managed to track down Paul Flick, her art professor at Glassboro State College, and wrote him a letter asking for an interview. A few weeks later I came home from school to find a note that my mother had left for me on the kitchen table. *Dr. Glick called you about a letter you wrote to him. He wants you to call him.* Joy was suddenly replaced by teenage angst. *Shit*, I thought, *how did she embarrass me when she spoke to this guy?* She even wrote his name incorrectly; it was Dr. Flick. Had she called him Dr. Glick? Did she engage him in conversation? This was turning into a nightmare.

Of course, I then had to withstand the bombardment of my mother's questioning after she arrived home from grocery shopping. "Who is this professor? Why did he call? Are you thinking about attending Glassboro? I thought you were going to Saint Joe's." And so the line of questioning went without even giving me time to respond until reprieve came from my seven-year-old brother who'd managed to get himself into trouble for which he needed my mother's help.

A few days later I drove to Glassboro for the interview. Dr. Flick was gracious and indulgent as he spent an hour remembering his former student, whom he described as "incredibly talented and restless." We toured the art rooms where she hung out; discussing her student art work and writing. I scribbled furiously into my notepad, trying to catch every word while also wanting to steep myself in the moment. Interview over, he walked me out into the brilliant sunlight. I turned to thank him. Backlit by the sun, he seemed to glow. "You take care. You are the first person to interview me about Patti. Good luck with your paper." (Year later Dr. Flick would be hit by a car and killed. He was just about to begin teaching Art Appreciation as an adjunct at a local community college. Coincidentally, I was hired as the adjunct to teach those courses.)

During my college years I dreamed of going to New York City to be a poet like Patti. Yes, I, an Italian-American teenager who commuted to a Jesuit college and worked in her father's pharmacy after school, wanted to live the bohemian life a la Patti Smith. I devoured her poetry and, living in pre-internet days, would trek to places like the Gotham Book Mart in New York City to buy her poetry books. She opened me up to other worlds and words. I was introduced to Arthur Rimbaud's *Illuminations* and *The Drunken Boat,* to the works of Paul Verlaine and William Blake. I wrote poetry while seated at the corner desk of my college's library. Words poured forth, words that enabled me to navigate the minefields of young adulthood.

And now, because my friend had gotten us tickets, I was going to finally see Patti perform live in a

Serendipity

small venue, the television studio of the Mike Douglas Show, filmed in Philadelphia, right across the river from my hometown. I pulled together my coolest outfit: black pants, black peasant top and, of course, the black ballet slippers. My friend and I were part of an audience comprised almost entirely of middle-aged women who adoringly laughed at everything said by James Brolin, the guest host. We sat through painfully long interviews of the other guests, Francesco Scavullo and Ruth Gordon. Then, nearing the end of the show, *she* was introduced. The curtain rose, and there stood Patti and her band. Waif-like, she was dressed in a white T-shirt and black pants; a red scarf was knotted around her neck.

She grabbed the microphone and ferociously belted out her first song, *Free Money*. Hard-driving, she claimed the stage. Her iconoclastic power and utter conviction were transfixing. I sat only a few feet from her. Raw and electrifying, she was mine. I didn't have to share her with any other fans. Trust me, nobody else in the audience except for my girlfriend and me knew who she was. As the icing on the cake, she sang *Ask the Angels*, one of my favorite songs.

After the show, the audience congregated outside, waiting to meet James Brolin. My girlfriend and I hung around hoping to see Patti. In her typical unassuming manner, Patti sauntered out of the studio like one of the audience members. I called her name and she turned in my direction.

"C'mon Patti," someone yelled from a waiting car. "We gotta get going."

"Hold on," she yelled back as she walked over to me.

"Hi," she said. "Did you call me?" Her speaking voice was quiet, almost childlike, nothing at all like the fist-pumping person I just saw perform her heart out.

"Yeah," I managed to get out of my mouth. "Can I take a picture with you?"

"Sure."

I handed my camera to my girlfriend. Patti put her arm around me. I tentatively put mine around her waist. *Holy shit,* I thought. *This is Patti Smith, right next to me.* She smiled for the photo and then jumped in the car. On the way home, I dropped the film off at the pharmacy to be sent out for processing. A week later, I opened the envelope and rifled through the now seemingly unimportant 23 images that had been on the roll, hoping that the last photo, the one of Patti and me, was there. This is an agony that we don't experience in today's age of camera phones and digital photography. Did the film develop? Did the picture take? There were no do-overs like there are with today's technology. Back then you just clicked and hoped. I came to the last photo, number 24. And there it was – one precious photograph of Patti and me. Patti, dressed in a black leather jacket and red scarf, has her arm around me, her hand resting on my left shoulder. My fist is raised, the beginning of defiance.

The trip to the Mike Douglas Show was transformational-a pilgrimage. I was young and impressionable. Patti opened me up to a world of possibilities through her music, her writings and, most importantly, an unwavering faith in self. Maybe more than the bohemian life, what I was longing to live was actually my own life, unfiltered, unbending to the rules of others as to how I should behave, how I should dress, and even to what I should aspire. *Aspire, not settle*-that became my mantra.

Meeting Patti Smith was a beginning. As I stood on the threshold of young adulthood, the seeds of challenge were planted. Young adulthood morphed into an early marriage that eventually transitioned into parenthood. During those years the challenges of raising a young family and subsequently navigating through an unexpected divorce dampened my spirit just a little. It took decades, but I regained my footing enough to feel that I was once again standing on solid ground and not the shifting sands that result from divorce.

Eventually, the rebuilding of my life expanded beyond returning full-time to the workforce and living on my own with two young children. I resurrected the spirit that was infused by the powerful messages of Patti Smith. Over the years she would reappear in my life whenever I needed her, a flesh-and-bone talisman. If I was in need of a psychic pep talk, I'd "happen" to hear one of her songs on the car radio. When I'd go to the bookshelf in need of some nighttime reading as I waited for one of my daughters to get home from work or a date, one of Patti's books would catch my eye. A few years ago, during one particularly stressful time, I saw that she was scheduled to give a reading at the Free Library of Philadelphia. And last year I took my daughters to hear her speak at another event at the Library. Her words, her gratitude for her gifts, her empowering message for the audience, and her powerful a cappella rendering of *Because the Night* were inspiring.

Patti Smith remains a reminder of the importance of not letting how others view or treat me define me or determine my course in life. I'm finding that as I grow older I am doing more releasing than ever before. I'm shedding things that no longer serve me; titles that don't really reflect who I am, people who drag me down rather than support me, and unneeded physical possessions. Through this most recent transformation and reworking of my life, Patti Smith remains a constant. Forty years after that first meeting she continues to shine a guiding light for

Serendipity

me. As a result of my pilgrimage to the Mike Douglas Show, I met my heroine; the one who encouraged and challenged me to dream big, have fun, follow my own calling, listen to my own voice, break confines, and always express myself, even if it gets me into fucking trouble.

Souvenir:

THE photo of Patti Smith and me that still is on my bedroom mirror (and on my kitchen cabinet, and in my office).

CHAPTER 2
SOUTH PHILADELPHIA AND SAINT RITA

Prayer is not an old woman's idle amusement. Properly understood and applied, it is the most potent instrument of action.

Mahatma Gandhi

The car pulls into my circular driveway in a hurry, gravel flying as it makes the turn around the pine trees. Engine running, he pushes open the passenger door. My daughters run out of the house.

Serendipity

Emily, calling "shotgun," attempts to snag the front seat. Alanna protests to her father, saying that her legs are too long to sit in the back seat. Her point has merit: she's 5'10." Alanna wins. Emily stomps around the car and slouches in the back seat. Doors slam shut. I hear the girls fighting as their father drives away with them. I heave a sigh; this is not how I thought my life would be, not in any nightmare scenario my mind might have conjured up. Divorced. Custody arrangements for the children. I wave until the car is out of sight-the car that I couldn't identify during the divorce proceedings when I had to inventory the assets.

"What's the make and model of your husband's car?" my lawyer asked.

"I don't know. He bought the car after he left. It's beige-colored."

"You don't know the make and model?" he asked again, this time a bit incredulously.

"No. I don't. I also don't know where he lives. Okay? Apparently there are a lot of things I don't know."

I slowly walk back to the house through the open front door-the one neither girl bothered to shut as they ran out. They always seem to be in a hurry. A few weeks earlier a boy came to pick up Alanna for a date. He honked the car horn and she scrambled to get her purse. I jumped off the couch, stopping her as her hand was on the doorknob.

"*Never* exit a house like that. Expect respect. He should turn off the damn car and have the decency to come to the door to get you. Now, wait."

"Mom, guys don't do that anymore. Geez. Why are you doing this?"

Alanna's cell phone rang. "My mom"-she drags out the word- "says you have to come to the door." She scowls at me as she holds the phone to her ear.

The boy obliges and knocks at the door. I greet him-and then they leave. I know I'm fighting a losing battle.

I grab my purse and car keys and set off for my monthly Saturday-night pilgrimage, which takes me across the Delaware River from New Jersey into South Philadelphia and to the Shrine of Saint Rita of Cascia. The seven-mile trip transports me back not only a century to when my grandparents worshipped at the church as children, but all the way back to early 15th-century Italy, to the town of Roccaporena, where Saint Rita, the Peacemaker, lived and died.

Tomaselli, Aita, Simone, Valente, Greco, Cerone, Rossi, Massa-great-grandparents on both sides of my family settled in South Philadelphia in the late 19th and early 20th centuries. Leaving behind Southern Italy, they moved to the neighborhoods already inhabited by the *comare* or *compare* who had also journeyed from the same regions in Italy-Benevento in Naples and Cosenza in Calabria. Arriving at the ports of New York and Philadelphia, their entry into America was eased by the welcome they received from those of their villages who had already settled in this country; ties to their *paisanos* with whom they shared homes, meals, and assistance in finding jobs remained unbroken.

Their Roman Catholic faith was part of the fiber of their lives. Their tiny three-story brick row houses were called Trinities or Father-Son-and-Holy Ghost. This style house was built to accommodate the lower classes. Often measuring only 16 feet across, the cramped houses originally only had one room per floor. Initially too poor to buy the houses, my ancestors were forced to rent from unscrupulous landlords who divided the already small homes into two-family dwellings. It was not uncommon for each of these families to have between eight and twelve children. Adding parents, grandparents, aunt, uncles, or other *paisanos* to the mix inhabiting these row houses made for an almost unbearable way of living. The row houses lined streets that were so narrow the wheels of a horse-drawn cart would scrape the pavement curbs.

These people were materially poor but rich in their devotion to the Catholic Church. The immigrant population was large enough for every neighborhood to support its own parish church: Saint Nicholas of Tolentine, Saint Paul, and the first

Italian-American parish in the country, Saint Mary Magdalen de Pazzi. The adjoining parish schools provided a formal education for the children, while classes in English were offered to the immigrant adults.

The Massa and Greco families (my paternal side) worshipped at the Church of Saint Rita of Cascia. Now designated a national shrine, the church was completed in 1907, a mere seven years after Rita was canonized. Designed to resemble a 14th-century Renaissance church, it was largely built by the Italian immigrants who populated the surrounding neighborhoods, their skills in stonework and painting still evident in the church. The painting on the dome above the marble altar depicts Saint Rita ascending into heaven. A century of smoke from the incense used during Mass has darkened the once vividly colored work. Pink marble columns flank the altar. Ornate sculptures of cherubs grace the altar's marble canopy. A large white marble statue of the saint stands in a marble scallop shell above the tabernacle. Two greater-than-life size white marble statues of angels, their wings meeting behind their heads, are positioned on either side of the altar.

I grew up in a tightly knit family, bound not only in our affection for each another, but also by our close physical proximity. No one moved out of the thirty-mile radius of the tri-state area of New

Serendipity

Jersey, Pennsylvania, and Delaware. Most Sundays we'd gather for dinner at the home of my paternal grandparents, Joseph and Anne, my namesake. Their house was a few blocks away from Saint Rita's church. It was the early 1960s and we still dressed up on Sunday. My father wore a suit and tie even if we weren't "visiting." My mother, Annette, was very fashion-forward and dressed in the latest mod styles. I remember how she daringly cut her hair short like Mia Farrow in 1967, the Summer of Love, during when my brother was born. My younger sister, Rosemarie, and I were always dressed in full slips, matching knit Piccolino dresses, and white patent leather shoes. My favorite dress was sunshine yellow and embroidered with large white daisies. We had spring and winter dress coats and hats, too, as well as white gloves and child-sized pocketbooks.

Working in a tiny kitchen measuring not more than 20 feet by 20 feet, my grandmother cooked her macaroni, meatballs, and gravy (red sauce). Lacking the now-standard kitchen essentials like granite countertops and stainless steel appliances, she managed to produce multi-course meals. She waited to boil the water for the macaroni until everyone had arrived. The aroma of the gravy simmering on a back burner greeted us as we walked through the front door. When my grandmother wasn't looking, we'd break off a piece of the crusty Italian bread and sneakily dip it into the gravy trying not to leave any tell-tale crumbs behind.

We hugged and kissed when entering and leaving the house. I remember bringing my "American" friends (as my grandmother referred to them) to Sunday dinner as a teenager. Forgetting to tell them of the kissing ritual, they'd stiffen as they were passed around to meet the family. And then the chorus of "Joe" would begin. My grandfather, father, brother, and cousin were all named Joseph. My paternal great-grandfather was also named Joseph-well, really he was named Giuseppe. To keep things straight, the Josephs were called Joe, Joey, Joseph, and Joe Baby.

Right before my grandmother would place Sunday dinner on the dining room table, my mother and aunt would help my sister, our cousin Regina, and me out of our dresses to save them from being bathed in gravy. I felt sorry for my cousin Tommy because he didn't get to undress. I guess that his white shirt and bow tie were easier to clean than our knit dresses. It was a special Sunday treat to be able to eat dinner in our white slips. Once in a while a rogue meatball might accidentally plop into our laps, but for the most part the slips remained white throughout the dinner. My grandmother would announce that dinner was ready and we'd assemble at the large wooden dining room table, the white tablecloth protected by a clear plastic overlay. She would proudly set the food on the table. My grandfather, seated at the place of honor at the head of the table, doled out the wine. We children always declined a little taste of wine, preferring the treat of soda.

We were the generation that rode in the back of station wagons, not only without seat belts but also without seats. We drank out of garden hoses and biked and roller-skated without helmets. So, it's no surprise that our parents propped us up on a few telephone books so that we could reach the table to eat. Once in a while a sudden movement by one of us would cause the pile of telephone books on the chair to shift, causing our elbows to bang onto the tabletop. An adult would calmly reposition the stack and dinner would continue. I was very proud of my ability as a seven-year old to balance on the telephone books while eating spaghetti that I learned to corral by twirling the fork and the pasta against the dinner plate. During the meal my grandmother would remind us that we were ladies (and a solo gentleman), so slurping of the spaghetti into our mouths was not tolerated.

We children would sneak a glance at the carved wooden sideboard that held dessert-an array of Italian cookies like pignoli dotted with pine nuts, butter cookies decorated with colored sprinkles (or "jimmies" as we called them), and bow-shaped fried cookies powdered with confectioner's sugar, as well as Anisette and other after-dinner liqueurs. Following dessert, my grandmother would bring out Pokeno (a game similar to bingo). There we'd sit, three generations, laughing, eating, and playing games. My grandparents' home held so many good memories for me as a child; it was a cocoon-warm, loving, nurturing, and safe.

The house was built in the late 1800s. My grandparents lived on the first floor. My grandfather, a stone mason, converted the second and third floors into large apartments, which were used as newlyweds by my parents and also by my aunt and uncle. My first husband, David, and I carried on the tradition, making the third-floor apartment our first home.

You could bet on two things in my family: no one moved away and no one got divorced. Until me-I did both.

David, and I met at eighteen as sophomores in college. He evolved into a very talented ceramic artist whose career took us to live in some unusual places, including a carriage house of an estate-turned-art center, where he was artist-in-residence, and an artist's colony in upstate New Jersey. We also found ourselves in Boulder, Colorado early in our marriage, where he attended graduate school. We moved back to New Jersey after his graduation when we found out that I was expecting our first child, Alanna. We wanted to raise the baby around family, most importantly around my grandparents. A few years later our second daughter, Emily Rose, was born.

When Emily was a toddler I began teaching Art History and Art Appreciation classes at local community colleges. It was a crazy time; some semesters I taught seven classes at three different colleges, but I liked the flexibility of my adjunct teaching schedule. I taught morning and evening classes and was able to be home during the day with the girls. My husband worked full-time as an art teacher and we juggled work schedules with the help of my parents. They watched the girls, feeding and dressing them, putting Alanna on the school bus, and entertaining Emily so that I could teach a morning class. The girls were indulged by their grandparents. I'd come home around noon to art projects sitting on the table and bread dough rising on the kitchen counter. David would get home in the late afternoon and we would pass the baton, or rather the children, as I exited for my evening class.

We were happy for a large part of our marriage, but now I realize that we had gradually been drifting apart, masking the alienation by the busyness of parenting young children. Things had gotten a little rocky soon after we purchased our first home, but I attributed it to nervousness over this big step. One day he left. Forever. Naïve as it sounds, I was blindsided-not to the problems in the marriage, but to the fact that he actually left and wanted a divorce. This was completely contrary to how I thought my life would play out. I thought we'd work things out, because, well, that's what you did.

We had just moved into our first home. Our dream home. It had everything we had been searching for-a lot of land in the town in which we wanted to raise the girls, a three-car garage where he could set up his ceramic studio and still be able to watch the girls play outside, and an apartment over the garage that could be turned into a gallery for his pottery. He had been my husband for 18 years. When he left, I was 41 and suddenly all by myself. I had never lived alone; I had commuted to college, living at home until I married at 22. I was scared: afraid of raising the girls without a father in the home, afraid of bills, and just plain afraid of bumps in the night. For the first few months after he moved out, I had the girls sleep in my bedroom on their mattresses which I had arranged on the floor, so I wouldn't have to sleep alone. But who was I kidding? I didn't sleep. I tossed, turned, worried, and cried.

During this trying time, I ached for something I couldn't have-the support of my grandparents, who had passed away. I wanted to be able to walk into their home-the solace of the familiar. My grandfather, Joe, was a short, stocky man. He was always

Serendipity

smiling-and smoking. His ever-present cigarette was his eleventh finger. When I'd visit he'd either be sitting on a chair in the parlor watching sports on television or, if the weather cooperated, he'd be sitting on a white metal chair in his prized rose garden in the postage stamp-sized yard, listening to the Phillies on the radio. My grandmother, Anne, was always girdled and well-dressed - in earrings, a necklace, and a pretty dress under her apron. I only saw her wear pants a few times in her life. If I didn't find her cooking in the kitchen or working in the garden, she'd be sitting on the yellow sofa, crocheting or reading. "Sit down, Miss Nan," she'd say, patting the space beside her. We'd talk about our days or watch one of her favorite television shows. After a while, I'd get up to leave. Removing myself from the sofa was hard for two reasons: I didn't want to leave my grandparents, and I had to break the suction between myself and the clear plastic that covered the sofa.

No longer able to physically visit my grandparents, I did the next best thing. I went to Saint Rita's. It soon became my refuge, a place where I could sit in spirit with my grandparents on the Saturday evenings that the girls were with their father. I'd ascend the steep white marble steps to enter the church, immediately comforted by being enveloped in the familiar setting. I'd settle into a wooden pew that had probably once held my grandparents. During Mass, I'd catch myself absentmindedly running my hand over the top of the pew, touching wood that others before me had held onto as they stood, knelt, and rose again during the service. Now only a handful of parishioners congregated for Saturday evening Mass, most of them elderly, the last remnants of a neighborhood whose demographics were shifting. But our voices rose in unison as we sang the hymns of praise.

One evening, having some time before Mass, I ventured down a narrow wooden side staircase, the steps rutted from over a century of use. A space to the right served as a statuary room. Large statues of saints, such as Saint Anne, stood on pedestals. Votive candles lit by the faithful flickered at the base of the statues. I was disappointed to see that real candles had been replaced by battery operated ones where you pushed a button to "light" the candle. I had always loved the ritual of lighting a candle, taking a long wooden stick that stood in sand next to the candles and touching it to the flame of an already lit candle in order to light my candle. I felt as if I was carrying on the chain of prayer by sharing the flame.

People wrote invocations on paper, placing them either at the feet of the statue or tucking them into the plaster folds of the statue's "garments." They resembled tiny white flags of surrender left by devotees releasing their problems to God. I felt a connection to these people who, like, me, had come to the shrine in

Serendipity

search of help, guidance, and comfort. I walked out of the statuary room and passed the gift shop that offered rosaries, holy water, holy cards, and holy oil.

Directly ahead was a circular room that was rather dark, devoid of natural light. A few people quietly milled around, reading wall plaques that told the story of the life of Saint Rita. A woman to my left knelt on a small red cushion in front of a tiny window, behind which was a gold cross. I kept my distance, respecting that she was engaged in prayer. She rose, blessed herself with the sign of the cross, and walked out of the room. Curious, I walked over to the window. A descriptive wall mount informed me that the golden cross behind the window held tiny relics of Saint Rita. A small wicker basket to the right of the window held folded pieces of paper, communications for the saint. Some papers were folded tightly but for those folded only once, the writings of the petitioners were visible. Some held prayers while others offered thanks for prayers answered.

I knelt in front of the relic, the very act of which released a sigh from deep within. Kneeling is an act of humility and, as I bowed my head in front of the relic, I offered up all of my pain and sorrow. I prayed for help. I prayed for hope. I prayed for guidance. I was such a mess. I had silently begun to cry. My nose was running. I reached into my coat pocket for a Kleenex but I could only find a dissolving wad of wet tissue that had long passed its useful (or identifiable) state. I continued to cry in silence, allowing the tears to cleanse me and release my fears and sadness. I then reached out, tentatively took a pencil, and wrote my petition to Saint Rita.

Please help my family and me.

It was as simple and as complicated as that. I looked around before placing the paper in the basket, wanting to be certain that no one was looking. I didn't want to appear needy, but that's exactly what I was. I was in need of reassurance that everything would be okay, that the pain would stop, that I could glue my family back together and, while we might not look exactly the same anymore, at least we would be whole again. I prayed. No, I pleaded-*help me, help me, help me*. The bells in the church above signaled the start of the Mass. I wiped my eyes, breathed deeply, and had faith that I was heard. I rose, making a quick stop in the restroom to compose myself before returning to the main church for Mass.

It was the first of many visits with Saint Rita. I began to use the shrine as I had used my grandparents' living room, as a place to sit in love. One day after Mass I noticed a pink paper next to the holy water font that announced the dates for the novena, or nine days of prayer, devoted to Saint Rita that would culminate in a day of Masses on her feast day, May 22. I noted the novena's start date and said the

Serendipity

special novena prayer every evening in my home just before bed for eight consecutive nights. I invoked Rita to help heal my broken marriage and family. On the ninth day, the last day of the novena, I made the pilgrimage to the shrine for the feast day Mass. This was not the Saint Rita's of the Saturday evenings I had come to know. Tour busses lined the street in front of the church. Hundreds of pilgrims filled the sidewalk. Some waited patiently to purchase roses from a makeshift tent on the sidewalk. Confused, I asked an elderly woman why they were selling roses. She said that red roses were the symbol of Saint Rita. Vendors were bundling the long-stemmed roses in newspaper and handing them to waiting customers. I bought a red rose and carried it into church.

The pews were packed; it was standing room only, everyone holding roses to be blessed. The altar had been transformed, overflowing with pink and red roses. I squeezed into a pew just as four men exited the sacristy carrying a large statue of the saint on a pallet that they supported on their shoulders. They encircled the church finally resting the statue to the left of the altar. At the end of the Mass Saint Rita's relics were brought to the front of the altar. People clogged the center aisle jostling for a chance to venerate the relic and then proceeded to the statue, against which they touched their roses. Over a thousand people would make the pilgrimage to the shrine on May 22. I had no idea that Saint Rita had so many devotees. Who was Rita? Why was she so beloved? I wanted to learn more about this woman, and after doing so, I know that I was led to this church and this saint by my grandparents for a reason.

Margherita Lotti, the woman who would become a saint, was born in Italy in 1381 in Roccaporena in Umbria, in the Republic of Cascia. Although attracted to a religious life as a young girl, she obediently entered into an arranged marriage at a very young age that produced two sons. Her husband was prone to anger, some of which was directed at Rita. Her husband was murdered, and Rita's sons wanted to avenge the death of their father to defend the honor of the family. Distraught over her husband's death, Rita did not want to see her sons drawn into an already violent situation. Hoping to calm the escalating tensions, she forgave her husband's murderers. Shortly thereafter, her two sons fell ill and died. Widowed and childless, Rita attempted to heed her earlier calling and enter the convent. The nuns initially refused her entry because relatives of her husband's murderers lived in the convent. Fearing that Rita's presence would create disharmony in the convent, she was turned away. Determined, Rita took it upon herself to broker a peace between the warring families. Her strength as a peacemaker was evidenced when the families signed a written agreement to end the vendetta. She then was granted entry to the convent, where she lived for over thirty years. Toward the end of her life she was visited by a relative who asked if she was in need of anything. Rita requested a rose from her family's garden. The relative returned to Roccaporena, and in passing the family's house, saw that a lone red rose was blooming in the snow on an otherwise barren bush. The red rose was brought to Rita. Now I understood why the pilgrims carried red roses.

I believe that my grandparents guided me to this shrine not only to place me in the hands of Saint Rita for the comfort for which I longed, but also to reveal to me lessons taught by the saint's life. Saint Rita continues to show me the importance of striving for peace at all costs, that harmony in life comes from dissolving the ego that sees everything and everyone as separate, that faith means surrendering to the love of God, and that peace is born within and manifests outward.

I continue to make the pilgrimage to Saint Rita's when I am in need of peace and quiet. Since that first visit over a decade ago, I continue to work on removing my ego as much as possible from the trying situation for which I'm asking for help and to release the petition without needing to control the details, trusting that I will be shown the way to broker a peace. I've used novenas to Saint Rita to ask for blessings for ill friends and relatives, ease with difficult situations, and strength for troubled loved ones. I've blended Saint Rita's messages with those from one of my other favorite saints, Francis of Assisi. *Make me an instrument of your peace.*

Lately the person I seem to be warring with the most is me. I ask Saint Rita to help me to be peaceful and patient with myself as I strive to move from a fear-based way of living to one of faith and trust. My prayers have not always been answered in the ways I might have hoped or specified. My first marriage was not saved, but my ex-husband and I remain on good terms. I now believe that prayers are answered in ways that are for the highest good of all involved. I've grown in my faith to trust that things are being done *for* me and not *to* me. Through my prayers I ask that my actions be guided and assisted for the good of all-whether it is parenting young adults, navigating relationships, or learning to be a little less judgmental of myself. Saint Rita never fails me. I thank my grandparents who I know guided me to her.

Amen.

Souvenirs:

Statue of Saint Rita.
Red rose from the novena.

CHAPTER 3
ENGLAND: FLIGHT OF FANCY

Humanity has advanced, when it has advanced, not because it has been sober, responsible, and cautious, but because it has been playful, rebellious, and immature.

Tom Robbins

My first act of rebellion came at the age of 44. I was always the good girl-the obedient one, the dependable one, the quiet one, still wearing the ghost of my parochial school uniform well into adulthood. I did everything by the book, even wearing that damned uniform-gold tie clasped, blue knee socks always pulled up, maroon vest buttoned atop the starched white blouse, polished sturdy blue shoes (referring to them as shoes is being complimentary; they were mini tanks).

I burdened my childhood self with such seriousness. No time to fool around like the other children. Little Annie was the go-to girl, the rule-follower, always on the "right" path, even if it wasn't hers. I never wanted to disappoint anyone. It didn't dawn on me until much, much later that I rarely, if ever, factored *me* into anything. I had become skilled at nudging myself out of my own life. Others before self. The cost? A life lived-I mean really lived, not just existing, following, and doing what others expected me to do.

Fun? I didn't need no stinkin' fun. I was reliable. I "sensibly" denied myself the opportunity to take risks, leap, fail and, worst of all, disappoint. I am a slow start; I'll grant you that. It may have taken me 44 years, but I was set to push some boundaries and break some rules, to risk disappointing others to please myself.

Emotionally and physically exhausted after my divorce, I found refuge in the bathroom, my favorite place to be alone and fall apart. Away from my two young daughters for a few minutes, I could turn on the faucet, lie in a heap on the floor, and cry. If I had time, I'd indulge in a snot-filled cry in the shower, hot water cascading over my body. Girlfriends tried to coax me into dating, but I just wasn't ready. I hadn't dated in over two decades. I didn't even know where to start. And I looked very different from when I last dated- in my teens. Thanks, but no thanks. I wasn't interested, and I certainly didn't have the energy to make myself presentable for a date or to even engage in small talk.

I masked my fear by stoically stating that I had to focus on rebuilding a nest for the girls. My excuse was that it was selfish to even be thinking of myself when my daughters needed me. I became a guilt-ridden mother who was pushing aside her own oxygen mask in order to parent. That just left the girls with a mother who was struggling to breathe, barely functioning, and certainly not living her life. One evening, the girls and I were snuggled on the couch watching the movie *E.T.* There's a scene near the end where E.T. is lying on the floor, a sickly shade of grey. Barely able to lift his "finger," he is dying. *That's me*, I remember thinking. *That's what I feel like. And I'm sure that's what I look like-that ghastly pallor.* I had large black circles under my eyes from lack of sleep. I barely had enough energy to lift myself off the couch. I felt like I was slogging through mud, moving through my life in slow motion.

And with much the same desire that I had that evening to reach into the television to help revive E.T., I promised myself that I would pick myself up and give to myself whatever I needed in order to get healthy and happy. I needed to end this period of mourning. I wanted to redefine myself, dropping all of the many labels I wore that were all variations of the words victim and martyr. After two years of living in a self-imposed state of denial, I washed my face, blew my nose, brushed my hair, and stopped taking so many showers.

I decided to start having fun. I began dating. Leaving the early dating disasters to another book, I'll tell you that I eventually met Martin, who would become my second husband. We clicked immediately. We liked the same music, beginning with the Ramones. On our first date, he spoke to me about his interest in the sun dagger petroglyph on Fajada Butte in New Mexico that marked the solstices and the equinoxes; pretty obscure, but coincidentally, something about which I taught in Art Appreciation class.

I put the poor guy through the wringer. I initially refused to tell him where I lived for fear that he was possibly a crazed ax murderer who might sneak into my home in the dead of night. I drove myself to our first dates, making sure to park far from the meeting location so he couldn't see my car and my license

Serendipity

plate, which he could use to trace me to my house. In hindsight, my behavior at the time sounds crazy. But life had proven to be not as predictable as I thought it was-or should have been. This time I was going to leave nothing that I could possibly control to chance.

As a product of an Italian-American upbringing, family came first-at all costs. The oldest of three, I married at the young age of 22, and before separation and divorce, I had been married for 23 years. My daughters were relatively young (10 and 13) when I began dating Martin three years after my marriage had ended. Everyone in the family seemed to be surprised that I was dating. I think the general consensus in my family, including for me as well, was that if I ever did date again, it would happen, oh, probably after the girls entered college in, say, five years. The unstated belief seemed to be that the girls had to come first, with me being a distant second. No, scratch that, not a distant second, it was as if my needs shouldn't factor into my life at all, at least not for the foreseeable future.

About a month after our first date I trusted Martin enough to give him my address. We realized that we only lived five miles apart. The distance to my parents' home was also five miles in the other direction. But the distance to visit Martin's parents was slightly further-3,000 miles further, which is why I traveled to England for the first time. I had only known Martin for two months when I decided to go abroad with him. By the time we landed in England, we had been dating for five months and I went from complete mistrust to boarding an international flight.

My mother especially was not supportive of my uncharacteristic decision. The acts of rebellion: getting my first passport, buying a plane ticket, leaving my daughters in the capable hands of their father, grandparents, and aunt, and getting on the plane to an overseas destination. Responses to the decision included:

"What's happened to you?"

"How can you leave the girls to spirit off to another country?"

"Overseas? What if the plane crashes?"

"Who's going to watch the girls while you're away?" (Hint: they have a father.)

"How can you be so rash?"

"Why do you have to go to England?"

"Have you lost your mind?"

No one understood that I hadn't lost anything. In reality I had found something: the courage (okay, the beginning of the courage) to live my life for myself. I was taking a step forward and, for goodness sake, the trip was only for fourteen days. Two whole weeks-such a short time really, but it was a long time coming. I was about to experience many firsts, my first international flight, my first extended time spent with Martin, and the first time I had ever left the girls.

With this decision, I found myself trusting again. I trusted that the plane would make it to and from England and that the wrath of God wouldn't be visited upon me for being self-centered. (I'm sure my fellow travelers would have been angry if they had become unknowing participants in my punishment.) I trusted that the girls would be well cared for (as past evidence could attest to) and that they might actually have fun for two weeks in the summer under the care of loving relatives. I trusted myself that I was making a good decision. You know the recipe: put in the ingredients of a healthier, happier me and produce a healthier, happier mother, daughter, and girlfriend. It was the first time I believed that I deserved to do something for me-without guilt. And, most importantly, it was the first time that I actually followed through. Although I had a destination (England) and a traveling companion (Martin), the trip was really about neither. Yes, I looked forward to getting to know Martin more deeply in the land of his birth. Yes, I looked forward to thoroughly enjoying my first taste of international travel. But the trip was really about me doing something for me.

I spent those two weeks in England taking care of myself. I had no responsibilities, no chores, no cares, no worries and, amazingly, no guilt. I had fun. I saw new things and met new people. I did everything I wanted to do when I wanted to do it. I purchased a calling card and spoke to the girls at least once a day. But, truth be told, they were usually having too much fun to want to come to the phone.

Vacations are finite by their nature, with beginning and end dates. This first visit to England lasted two weeks. But the effects of the visit were long-lasting. It was the start of a deeper self-knowing, a time where I engaged in an uninterrupted dialogue with myself. I lived more in the present than I tended to do at home, enjoying where I was and who I was with without another task to attend to or another errand to run. After this first trip to England, travel became a necessity, not a luxury. I physically traveled to England. But, in hindsight, it was the start of traveling to Self. Yes, that Self, the one that commands a capital letter. Six months earlier I would have thought you were crazy if you told me that I'd be vacationing in England with my boyfriend.

Martin hailed from South Yorkshire. Whenever he would bring me flowers on our first dates they would be white roses.

"What's up with the white roses?" I jokingly asked. "Do you have some sort of a prejudice against the red ones?"

Serendipity

"You're kidding, right?" he responded. "Don't you know about the Wars of the Roses?"

With a sneaking suspicion that he wasn't talking about the Michael Douglas movie, I had to admit that I wasn't well versed in his country's internal strife.

"The white rose is the symbol of the House of York, the red rose is the symbol of the House of Lancaster," Martin explained. "They were rival dynasties. I'm from Yorkshire, so white is the only acceptable color of rose for me," he joked. (I think.)

At our wedding a few years later, I carried a bouquet of white roses and had a white rose sewn onto my gown.

I arrived in England on what would have been my 22nd wedding anniversary, the final bit of closure on my first marriage. If I closed my eyes, I could still see a young woman entering a church to meet her groom, nervously clutching a bouquet of calla lilies, wearing her mother's wedding gown. And now I found myself in another country, far from home, sitting in the yard of Martin's parents. Jet-lagged, I sunk into the lawn chair, feeling the warmth of the sun (surprisingly, there was sun in England that afternoon), thinking how far I had come, literally and figuratively. Life doesn't go according to plan, I thought, much as I had admitted a few years earlier at the time of my separation from my then-husband. This time my response, however, was "and that's okay." It felt surreal to actually be in England. I ground the toe of my sandal on the lawn, needing to make sure this was real and not a dream. I had actually done it.

Martin's parents had created a beautiful English garden. Hydrangea of different varieties bloomed in the backyard, snowball-size blossoms of bright blue sharing space with a lilac-colored, lace-cap variety. Although small, the yard also had a tree laden with apples, miniature roses, and a tiny greenhouse filled with tomato and cucumber plants. My eyes followed the runner beans working their way up a trellis along the red brick wall. The chimney caps on the roofs of the neighboring houses appeared to be made of clay, each unique in its design.

Soon Martin's friends began flocking to the backyard much like the starlings flying overhead. They introduced themselves with their broad Yorkshire accents, which at times were hard to understand. "Eyup, Martin. Is this your lass?" I took off my sunglasses and cast Martin a wide-eyed, *please translate for me* look. Martin leaned to me. "They said, hello, Martin. Is this your lady?" Seeing I was tired from the jet lag (I'm certain that my nodding head was a telltale sign), they mercifully focused their conversation on Martin. I put my sunglasses back on so I could close my eyes for a bit without feeling that I was being rude to his *mates* who had come to welcome his

Serendipity

American *bird* (girlfriend). Martin helped them understand that I needed to *kip* (nap) because I was *knackered* (tired) from the transatlantic flight.

Martin and I decided to have no itineraries, no planned-out days. Each day we selected a new town to visit based on what we read about the evening before in some books his parents had, recommendations from his family, or because Martin wanted to take me someplace special to him, like Lincoln, where he had attended college. I didn't want to treat the travel as I did my work-with goals, to-do lists, and structure: in doing so, my boundaries naturally expanded.

We visited the Yorkshire Dales, whose valleys were carved by ancient glaciers. Sheep and cattle dotted the steep green pastures, kept from the roads by hand-built dry stone walls. We traveled to Derbyshire in the Peak District, visiting the quaint town of Bakewell. (Okay, all towns in England are quaint.) I had asked Martin to take me there after reading about the pudding for which the town was known.

We parked in a lot next to a creek. An elderly man dressed in a sweater and flat cap was feeding ducks as children scampered along the creek's bank. Crossing a stone bridge, we walked right into a baking rivalry, two shops both claiming to be the purveyor of the original Bakewell pudding. We naturally had to try one from each shop, availing ourselves of a double dose of the egg and ground almond confection. On a bit of a sugar high, Martin and I took a sprightly walk across town to look at the well dressings for which Derbyshire was renowned.

Derbyshire continues a summer tradition of decorating and blessing water sources such as wells. Probably pagan in its roots, well dressings were revived during the bubonic plague. Martin and I walked over to a white tent where three teenage girls stood over a table finishing well dressings. I watched as one girl, a redhead, blew hair out of her eyes as she pressed natural materials such as flower petals, beans, pods, and seeds into a wet clay tablet to create a still life. Two other girls were bent over their clay slab, intently creating a religious-themed well dressing. Martin slipped his hand in mine. Nodding in the direction of the well dressing, he winked. "Not too shabby, huh?" I leaned my head onto his shoulder and watched as the girls finished up their work.

Over a glass of shandy at an outdoor café, I asked Martin if we could take the short drive to Eyam. Having just finished reading *Year of Wonders* by Geraldine Brooks, I wanted to visit the town that became known for its self-sacrifice in the late 1660s as the bubonic plague swept through England. Martin was keen on going because he was interested in the village from a scientific standpoint. He had read

Serendipity

that the plague was not transferred to some villagers who cared for victims, leading to 20th-century research that determined that some people carried a gene that made them immune to the plague. We drove through the undulating hills of the Dales into the tiny town of Eyam, one led there by her heart, the other by his mind.

The bubonic plague was brought to Eyam in 1665 when a flea-infested bolt of cloth was delivered from London to the local tailor. It ravaged the village for 14 months, killing three-quarters of the inhabitants, sometimes wiping out entire families. Martin parked the car and wanted to go to straight to the museum that told the story of the plague, including that of the DNA research. I told him I'd meet up with him; I wanted to walk the streets of the town.

Twenty-first-century residents now occupied the town's small stone row houses in which the plague traveled so quickly and indiscriminately 450 years earlier. Each well-maintained home had a small front garden. At some houses summer flowers in window boxes shared garden space with children's toys, push chairs (strollers), and tricycles. The sight made for a strange juxtaposition, as many of the cottages were also marked with plaques recording the names and dates of death of the victims who had died within their walls.

I paused in front of what had at one time been the home of the Hancock family. Only one member of this family of eight survived the plague-Mrs. Hancock, wife and mother. She unknowingly brought the plague to her family by having assisted with the burial of a friend who was a victim. Unbelievably, she buried her entire family of six children and husband in a span of eight days. I had a sudden longing to hug my own children who were back home in New Jersey. Resisting the familiar tug of guilt, I reminded myself that I wasn't in England to escape my family; I was there to find me.

I mourned with Mrs. Hancock, who, not wanting to expose others to the ravages of the plague, chose to bury her children and husband without any assistance, digging the graves herself. What did she think on her walk back to her home after another burial to tend to the other sick members of her family? What did she do when she finally closed the door behind her, having buried the last of her family, alone, no one left to tend to? She became a heroine to me for her selfless devotion to her family.

Martin caught up with me and we walked through the church graveyard, the final resting place of some of the early plague victims. (As the plague progressed, the villagers stopped burying the dead in the church graveyard. Burials were relegated to one's own yard or the outlying fields.) We were quiet as we read the epitaphs. Finally, Martin broke the silence. "So these are the people that I just read about in the exhibition," he said somberly. Some tombstones were very large and elaborate, like that of wife of the rector, William Mompesson. These stood in stark contrast to the smaller gravestones with their primitively carved images of skulls and crossbones that gave testament to the grim reaper. Differentiation between and rich and poor seemed to continue even in death, except for the irony that the plague knew no social and economic boundaries.

Reverend Mompesson had led the villagers in a self-imposed quarantine in an attempt to stop the spread of the plague to other villages. Ironically, this isolation may have led to more deaths in the village because people remained in close proximity to each other. However, more than being known as the Plague Village, the village became known for its self-sacrifice, most likely sparing other villages a similar fate. With access to food and medicine curtailed, the townspeople of Eyam came to depend on the humanitarianism of neighboring villages.

"Let's take a walk to Mompesson's Well," suggested Martin. He took my hand as we left the graveyard to walk the footpath that eventually led us out of the village proper and up a hill. At the top of the hill was the well where the residents of Eyam would leave coins in jars of vinegar in return for supplies left by neighboring villagers. Such selflessness on either side of the well caused me to question if I would have been willing to have been one of the unsung heroes of Eyam or its neighboring villages. I turned to Martin. "What would you have done? If you lived in a nearby village would you risk contracting the plague to bring supplies to the well?"

He held his hand to his chin as he thought. "Yeah, I think I would have. How could I not? They would have starved without the supplies because they willingly shut themselves off from the other villages to stop the spread of the plague."

"What about you, Anne?"

I wasn't proud of the hesitancy or of the first response that came to mind. "Probably," I responded. I was too embarrassed to tell him the truth which was that I didn't think that I would have risked my own health or that of my family to bring the supplies.

Martin and I parted, each walking a short distance in different directions. The beauty of the landscape, a patchwork of varying shades of green, played off against the emotional heaviness that I felt at the well. I came upon a small gathering of headstones surrounded by a low dry stone wall. Over the years wind and rain had chipped away at the writing on the headstones. Moss on the headstones created a pattern through which I tried to read the faded words. One headstone read "Alice Hancock,

Serendipity

1666." I had come upon the final resting place of the Hancock family, unknowingly walking the same path that Mrs. Hancock followed seven times that August. As I stood there I silently offered Mrs. Hancock my hand to hold, my shoulder to cry on. Suddenly the real answer to Martin's question rose from within, without hesitation.

Yes, I would have brought supplies to the villagers.

I called Martin over to see the graves. He leaned over the wall in an attempt to read the headstones. As he stepped back, I put my arms around him from behind. "It's so indescribably sad. The plague might have taken her family, but it couldn't take away her love for them," I said, as I pulled Martin closer. I knew how important my family was to me. I knew that Martin felt the same way. I was reminded of the transience of life; that each and every moment together is precious and to be appreciated, even those frustrations that I sometimes felt raising teenagers. It's all part-and-parcel. Evening was beginning to fall as we headed back home, Bakewell pudding in hand, a teatime treat for his parents.

I soon came to experience that Northern England's landscape could be both breathtakingly beautiful and starkly uninviting. Some days the Yorkshire sky would be sapphire blue, dotted with white wisps of clouds. Many times, though, the landscape was grey as if some unimaginative child colored an entire page of a coloring book in that shade with different tones – wool, rainstorm, flannel, dove, Wall Street, shadow (only Benjamin Moore could be imaginative enough in paint naming to make grey appealing). Grey sky, grey stone buildings, and grey stone walls. It was grey and cold even in August. Fireplaces took no summer vacation; Martin's aunt kept her charcoal fire burning all year.

One day we decided to visit Haworth, a town bordering the West Yorkshire Moors. We drove through hills that gradually transitioned into craggy limestone outcroppings, an area that grew more desolate with each passing mile. Perched at the top of a steep hill, Haworth is situated in the Pennines, a mountain range referred to as the backbone of England. There was an emotional heaviness to Haworth. The sky was dark and stormy on the day we visited. The wind was fierce and cut right through me. While the open doors of the gift shops and tea shops beckoned to me, the landscape itself was not welcoming and seemed to be asking me not to stay. Haworth's narrow main street, lined with stone buildings blackened by hundreds of years of soot and ash, is relatively unchanged from when the Bronte family settled there in 1820.

This was the village where Emily, Anne, and Charlotte lived and wrote, and their brother, Branwell, drank at the local pub, The Black Bull.

Serendipity

Though stark and desolate, the area provided inspiration for the Bronte sisters. Emily set *Wuthering Heights* on the nearby moors; Charlotte used a neighboring village as the setting of *Jane Eyre*. It's hard to imagine how the Bronte sisters could have written anything other than dark works in this bleak and windswept village. The family came to the town when their father, Patrick, a pastor, took over the parsonage. Maria, Patrick's wife, had given birth to four children in the four preceding years. Sadly, Maria died the year after the family settled in Haworth.

The remoteness of the town resulted in an isolation that served as a catalyst for the family's closeness. The sisters tended not to interact too much with the locals, preferring the company of each other to those outside of the family.

Martin and I toured the Bronte home, a surprisingly warm, inviting space with small but well-appointed rooms. Three of the siblings, Branwell, Emily, and Charlotte, died in the house. However, the home wasn't all dour and death. I could feel the happy presence of the sisters in the dining room. The caretaker shared that the three sisters would walk around the dining room table in the evenings reading their works aloud to each other, which often resulted in spirited conversation. I thought of my own family back home, how my daughters and I had also created our own safe and warm space in which to grow, laugh, and love.

The Black Bull pub, which had a commanding presence at the top of the village's main street, stood almost directly in front of the church where Pastor Bronte preached. Hanging baskets of bright red geraniums provided a vibrant pop of color against its darkened stone façade. Martin and I stepped into the pub for a bite to eat. I slid into a red upholstered window seat while Martin chose a chair opposite me at the table for two. I placed my purse on the stone floor and picked up a menu.

On my travels to England I discovered that the country's eating establishments all too often lacked two of my much-needed drinking accessories-ice and straws. I'm constantly perplexed by how little the English use ice in their drinks. I thought I had discovered a savvy way to enjoy more than the pathetic two cubes that would be floating in my Diet Coke by also asking for a glass of ice on the side, only to find that the side glass usually contained about three extra cubes. Now, there's no shortage of water in England and also no recipe for making ice, so I remain confused. (I've also never stayed in a hotel in England that has an ice machine.) There also seems to be a shortage of drinking straws in restaurants and even fast food places. I got up from the table and approached the bar to ask for a straw for my soda. A child came up behind me and I waved her on ahead of me. She asked for a straw which the man behind the bar produced.

"I'd like a straw, too," I said.

"Sorry," he replied. "That was the last straw."

"You're kidding, right?" I asked, looking around for a hidden camera, thinking I was on the English version of Candid Camera.

"No, sorry, that was the last one."

Shaking my head, I returned to the table to drink my warm soda without a straw and ice.

After lunch we did a bit of window shopping before taking a final walk around the church just as the sun was setting. The building was backlit by an orange sky: the flag of England with its red cross against a white background flapped in the brisk wind. The tower's clock told us that we should be getting back home for teatime with Martin's parents.

Yorkshire is often described as "God's Own Country," partly because of the vast, unspoiled areas of the Yorkshire Dales and the North York Moors. Martin and I were visiting England in August because of his teaching schedule. We were treated to the beauty of the rolling hills dotted with purple heather that was then at its peak. While breathtakingly beautiful, some of the areas are also very remote, with harsh climates. A few days after our trip to Haworth, Martin decided to take me to the seaside, as he called it. We drove through the North York Moors, an expanse of land endless as far as the eye could see, stretching through vales to the coast of the North Sea. We got out of the car to stretch our legs at the top of the Hole of Horcum, a 400-foot hollow that's almost a mile wide. Hikers made their way along established routes cut into the landscape. As it was late summer, the heather blanketed the moors in a (pardon me) purple haze. White sheep grazed in the distance among the heather. Shadows cast from the billowy clouds looked like paper cut-outs on the valley floor. Although the hills undulated, there was nothing soft about the landscape. The moors are formidable; it's no wonder that they have a role in *Wuthering Heights*, *Dracula*, and even the film *An American Werewolf in London*.

We drove a little further before Martin parked at an overlook so that I could stand on the crest of the moors and catch my first glimpse of the North Sea and the fishing town of Whitby in the distance. The remains of Whitby's abbey are perched high on a cliff, its stone arches devoid of stained glass. Whitby was my first encounter with the English seaside. The muddy, pebbly beaches were uninviting to this New Jersey girl accustomed to sitting on a white sandy beach on a hot summer afternoon. Cold, with only a few children venturing into the sea, people were huddled behind windscreens, bundled up

Serendipity

against the wind and sea spray on this late August afternoon. The sounds of the beach, though, were the same – children laughing, seagulls calling, ice cream vendors ringing bells. As we walked the pier, Martin told stories of childhood seaside visits including watching Punch and Judy puppet shows on the beach.

"Would you like to take a donkey ride?" Martin asked.

"Are you propositioning me in some weird way?" I responded.

"That's funny, but no," he said, gesturing to the donkey giving rides to children on the beach, an English seaside staple.

"No, thanks," I said. "But I'd love to go shopping!"

Stores competed for the sale of jewelry made with what I mistook for onyx. Martin explained that it was really jet, a form of fossilized wood found primarily in Whitby's cliffs. He steered me into a small jet shop and asked to see the rings. He picked up a silver ring with an intricate Celtic design inlaid with jet. "Anne, I'd like you to have this," he said, holding the ring out for me. "I want you to always remember this trip." I took the ring and put it on my finger. He slipped his arm around my waist and guided me along the town's narrow cobblestone streets.

While taking a Sunday afternoon ride a few days later, Martin and I happened by chance upon the tiny village of Hooton Pagnell. First mentioned in the Domesday Book, a 1086 survey of England ordered by William the Conqueror, it has a population of around 200 people. Hooton Pagnell is an estate village, with many of the homes still owned by the estate's owner. The open door to Hooton Pagnell Hall, the estate's main house, which dates back to the 14th century, caught my attention. I asked Martin to stop the car so I could explore. I crossed the threshold to sneak a quick peek at this privately held space and was greeted by a large gabled house flanked by trees. Immediately transported back to another time, a small part of me expected to see a knight rounding the corner.

I found myself photographing a lot of thresholds while in England-doors that were open or doorways that led to another space. I wasn't interested in photographing the beautiful, old, intricately carved closed doors that I saw on castles or in tiny alleys or on churches. The open doors were friendlier, as if I were being invited into spaces beyond. I remembered reading that a scientific study found that crossing thresholds causes us to forget, something about the mind filing away memories once we walk through a doorway. Forgetting. Maybe the tradition of crossing the threshold as a newlywed was meant to cause one to forget one's life before marriage. Maybe my attraction to thresholds in England was a signaling to me that I was beginning a new phase of my life. When one door closes and another one proverbially opens; we are meant to move fully through the door, not straddle the threshold. Maybe the cliché is true; that is, if we were meant to look behind, we would have been born with eyes in the back of our heads.

For the remainder of our visit we continued to tour the countryside, trying to make it back home each day by teatime to eat with Martin's parents. I marveled at the simplicity of their evening meal-eggs, bread, cheese, a few slices of meat, spring onions, and tomatoes-followed by a piece of cake or a biscuit (cookie). The four of us sat around the tiny kitchen table. There was a little small talk about our day, mostly between Martin and his mother. His father was a quiet man.

I liked to walk the narrow streets of Martin's childhood village and snuck away a bit each day to do so. It was a mining town, cloaked in a no-nonsense feeling. The austerity brought on by both World Wars was still very much present. Most of the houses had their front metal fencing cut to the nubs, a reminder of how the wrought iron had been needed during the First World War. The stone row houses were still marked by the soot of coal fires from long ago. It was a small village set in a rolling countryside. I found myself making excuses to go out on walks alone. I'd volunteer first thing in the morning to walk to the neighborhood cooperative down the street to buy the newspaper. The mornings were quiet and unrushed; I cherished this time, finding it such a luxury to be able to take a morning stroll alone.

On some of my solo walks I'd watch the white clouds move in over the hills. I might glance into the window display of the butcher shop with rows of pork pies and garlands of sausages. Other times I'd mail some postcards in the round, cherry-red post box with the gold insignia of the Queen. On one particularly long walk I ended up at the tiny church of Saint Helen, where Martin had served as an altar boy in his youth. I was now able to place where I saw him in a black-and-white photo as a child, dressed in a cassock and white surplice.

At twilight, I'd stand at the top of a street as the darkness of night was pulled over the town below, watching as house lights turned on, tiny dots against the evening sky marking where families were returning home. I'd offer to give Martin and his parents some time to talk in the kitchen after dinner, really wanting an excuse to take a walk up the hill to visit the cemetery. Some headstones were so old that identities were lost, names eroded by the weather. Others told sorrowful tales of lives ended too soon. These were Martin's people, his roots, and his stock-something that the Martin I met in America lacked. Martin became complete to me in England. I had a

Serendipity

wonderful time with him as our relationship blossomed. His eagerness to introduce me to his family, his friends, and his country was so endearing. Our relationship grew during that trip, and two years later we would return to England for our honeymoon.

On my last evening in England I look a final walk alone as Martin gathered up some family photographs to take back to America. I strolled for about thirty minutes before turning back in the direction of the house. I cut through the snicket (the alley) and arrived back at his parents' home. I could see Martin's father in the tiny greenhouse in the backyard, gathering some tomatoes for teatime. Having spent his entire life in the coal mines, he walked a bit hunched over, moving slowly, checking each plant. I paused at the front gate where Martin once posed in a black-and-white photograph on his first day of school, wearing his grammar school "boy's cap" and blazer with school insignia. I walked through the gate. Looking through the window I saw Martin's mother in the kitchen boiling water for tea. She moved to the tiny, apartment-sized refrigerator tucked in the pantry to retrieve a pork pie. A faded flowered cloth covered the small square table that had been set for four. They had made a place for me at the table and in their lives.

The moments that grew into pilgrimage came from the times that I spent with myself. The seemingly mundane walks that I took alone around Martin's village transformed into walking meditations. It was becoming apparent to me that, through this physical separation from my life in the United States, that I was beginning to become a whole person, not a compilation of discrete pieces: a piece of a daughter, a piece of a mother, a piece of a girlfriend, and a piece of a sister. The trip offered me the time and space that I never permitted myself back home. As I look back on that first real flight and subsequent forays back to England, I realize that I continue to be on a pilgrimage to that sacred place called Soul as it's slowly being revealed that I have within me the very things that I've been leaving home to find.

<u>Souvenirs:</u>

Tea towels of all of the places I visited. I don't use them; I store them and take them out every once in a while to look through them as some sort of fabric postcards. We bring the same ones back for Martin's mother. She uses them.

Leather bookmarks that I buy at all of the gift shops. Back home I like to choose which one is most appropriate for the book I'm reading.

A copy of *Wuthering Heights*.

The silver and jet ring.

CHAPTER 4
THE RIVER MERSEY

So ferry 'cross the Mersey
'cause this land's the place I love
and here I'll stay.

Gerry Marsden

This is no beautiful river, at least not from where I stand on its banks at Liverpool's Albert Dock. It's an industrial river with a no-nonsense purpose of transport to and from the Irish Sea; a blue-collar river, if rivers have such distinction. To me, the River Cam surrounding Cambridge University is a white-collar river, a river of leisure, hosting pleasure boats. The River Mersey seems to have no time for such frivolity.

Anne Greco

The water is grey today, mirroring the sky above. The fast-moving current forms white caps as it flows to the sea. A strong wind tugs at the hood of my jacket like a schoolboy mischievously trying to grab it. The River Mersey has a siren's call to me. I journey to the Mersey whenever I'm in England, lured by a force I can't resist nor explain. When I stand next to the Mersey, I feel that I've come home. My soul is fed by its sight. My body calms, my mind quiets, and I am at peace.

Liverpool, nestled against the river's banks, is the home of the Beatles, the Cavern Club, the Cunard Building, and the Tate Liverpool. Its list of attractions is impressive. Yet, during my visits, I find myself literally turning my back on the city to stand at the river's edge. Looking across to the town of Birkenhead, I notice the ferry has just docked there, commuters disembarking at the end of their workday. This is the ferry made famous in the Sixties by the Gerry and the Pacemakers' song, "Ferry Cross the Mersey." I first heard the tune played on the jukebox in the luncheonette next to my father's business, Packer Park Pharmacy. Six years old at the time, I never could have known that one day I'd visit the river in England. It was 1965 and my family was living in South Philadelphia. On rare occasions, my mother would allow me to walk to visit my father at work and then eat at the luncheonette next door. Although we only lived a block from the pharmacy and there

Serendipity

was no street to cross, I felt like a big girl making the trip solo. I was allowed to order lunch for myself and pick my own songs from the jukebox. My wings were only slightly clipped by needing to be helped onto the lunch counter stool on which I'd spin until my food arrived. I'd eat my hoagie with legs kicking to my jukebox selections of Gerry and the Pacemakers followed by Petula Clark singing "Downtown."

But I digress. Back to England and how I first encountered the Mersey. I took three trips to England before I finally visited Liverpool. On our annual trips to visit Martin's family, we tended not to have too much of an itinerary. Wanting to be home with his parents most evenings for teatime, we'd look at a map and take daytrips to places that struck our fancy. An early riser, I usually had the house to myself before I heard the stirrings of my in-laws and then, much later, my husband, who was still claiming jet lag almost a week after our arrival. The corner of the small parlor in my in-laws' house held a bookshelf and a high-backed chair. Martin's family refers to this corner as the library. The shelves mainly hold books on subjects related to England, like the royal family, rugby, and English history. One morning while flipping through a book on English landscapes, the sites of Liverpool caught my attention. Since my brother and his sons are Beatles fans, I thought that Martin and I could visit Liverpool and I could also do some early Christmas shopping. I proposed the trip to Martin and a few hours later we had booked a hotel for a two-night stay.

The two-hour highway drive from Martin's hometown of Hoyland Common to Liverpool was nothing to write home about. As we entered the city limits, we were met with the sights of run-down houses, warehouses, and vacant storefronts. We wound through the blighted and industrial part of the city until finally turning onto the street fronting the docks that date from the 1800s-Prince's Dock, Albert Dock, and George's Dock. The Cunard Building on George's Dock still stands as testimony to Liverpool's prominence in the 19th-century shipbuilding industry. The Liver Building (pronounced *ly-ver*) is next to the Cunard Building; its two towers, with clock faces larger than those of Big Ben, are topped by 20-foot statues of the mythical liver birds from which the city derives its name.

Our hotel was a converted 19th-century warehouse. Our room faced the Albert Dock, a complex of century-old red brick warehouses that now house bars, restaurants, offices, and retail shops. Tourists wandered in and out of the stores, but the river that flowed about twenty feet below the hotel's walkway kept drawing my attention. Over the next two days Martin and I walked the city, learning more about Liverpool's historical ties to shipbuilding and its

Serendipity

more contemporary ties to British Invasion music. I shopped at the Beatles Story. Martin wanted to tour the Tate Liverpool art museum on Albert Dock. I looked through the glass façade to see the amazing art beckoning. But the squawking of gulls pulled my attention to the river. I asked Martin if he minded touring the museum alone because I wanted to sit next to the river instead. He looked at me quizzically.

"Anne, it's the Tate. What are you thinking? You teach Art History. What do you mean you want to sit by the river?"

"I don't know, Martin. I just want to sit outside and watch the river. I don't want to be cooped up inside right now. You go. I'll be fine."

I waved him on to the art treasures, quite content to sit next to something that I found equally as spectacular. I walked until I found some steps to sit on near the ferry station. The dock was busy, filled with people strolling among the shops, hurrying to catch the ferry, or pausing to eat an ice cream cone pierced with a Cadbury Flake chocolate bar. After doing a bit of people watching, I shifted my attention to the Mersey. A few months earlier I had been introduced to the practice of open-eye meditation during a workshop. I learned how to enter into a state of relaxation by focusing on something physical like the flame of a candle or by repeating a mantra. I set the timer on my phone to 15 minutes, inhaled deeply and then exhaled all of the air from deep inside my lungs. I settled into my seat. My gaze focused on the Mersey. My mind settled, and slowly the distractions of the people dissolved. After what only seemed like a few minutes, the chiming of the phone's timer brought my attention back to the dock where I was sitting. I stood up, stretched, mouthed a thank-you to the river, and then walked back to the Tate to find Martin.

On our last evening in Liverpool we dined al fresco at a pub on the dock. I had my standard shandy and scampi, while Martin chose a stout and steak-and-ale pie. The gulls circled between the river and the diners, on a constant lookout for food. The sky turned a pinkish-orange color as the sun began to set. It was that time of evening when everything seems to take on a soft glow. The yellow lights of the clocks on the Liver Building turned on, the statues of the liver birds silhouetted against the evening sky. Night was drawing over the river that remained steadfast in its movement to the sea.

As we left Liverpool on that first visit, I craned my neck to have a final view of its river. I thought about asking Martin to turn the car around, not wanting to leave the river behind. But I wasn't yet ready to share with Martin the captivation the river held for me, because I couldn't yet explain it to myself. I knew it would be at least a year before I'd be

Serendipity

able to meet up with it again, so I purposely left a piece of my soul with the River Mersey-knowing that I'd have to return at some time to retrieve it.

Back home in the States, I eventually shared my connection to the river with Martin and my two daughters. Emily was still living at home and so heard more of the tales of the river than did Alanna, who was away at college. I thought a lot about this one-of-a-kind deep experience with the Mersey and gradually moved beyond thinking with my rational mind to feeling that the connection existed on a much deeper level. A year later Martin and I returned to England and the Mersey. This time, though, I rode the ferry for the first time, needing to make one call from its deck, to Emily. She was in the produce aisle of a grocery store in New Jersey when her phone rang.

"Emmy, guess where I am?" I shouted, partly in excitement and partly to be heard above the wind.

"Mom, I can barely hear you. Where are you?"

"The ferry, Emmy. I'm on the ferry crossing the Mersey. I'm doing it!"

"Yeah! I'm so happy for you, Mom. See it for me, but don't start singing that song," she laughed referring to "Ferry Cross the Mersey."

We hung up. Martin turned to go inside the ferry, motioning for me to join him. I waved him on, unwilling to leave the river. It was cold and the wind was ferocious. Although I was getting wet from the Mersey's spray, I stood on the deck as the ferry moved through the river, breathing in the river's majesty.

I recently made my first trip back to the Mersey in four years. Martin and I checked in to our favorite hotel on Albert Dock, where I had requested a room with a river view.

"Are you certain it's the river view you want?" the receptionist asked. "Most people want the view with the docks and the Liver Building."

"No, river view, please."

I sat in front of the window while Martin went to get us some take-away food. The weather was wretched for both days that we were there-grey skies and cold, windswept rain. We slogged through the rain to do a bit of shopping, dining, and general reacquainting ourselves with the wonderful city. During a brief reprieve from the rain, Martin voiced a desire to go to the Mersey Maritime Museum. He stopped himself mid-sentence and looked at me.

"Let me guess? You want to sit by the river?"

"Yep. Do you mind going alone?"

"Anne, I accepted years ago that I need to share you with the Mersey."

The steady rain had lessened to a drizzle. I took a hand towel from the bathroom to dry the metal bench in front of the hotel. The coldness of metal made its way through my summer cotton pants. I zipped up my jacket and pulled the hood close to my

Serendipity

head. And I sat. And I sat. And I sat. In pure bliss. A soft drizzle continued to fall. People with umbrellas slowed a bit as they passed, looking at me quizzically. The sky grew darker and the water churned. The Mersey seemed to be in hurry and a tad bit angry. But it was all good. I knew that the agitation was only on the surface, and that deep below the water was calm. In the distance I could see the ferry slowly crossing the river, making its way from Birkenhead to Liverpool. It was as if I had never left the Mersey. It felt so good to be back "home."

I noticed that since my last visit people had begun to put locks on the railings surrounding the docks. Some locks had the names of lovers written on them, others had endearing messages. I was sorry that I didn't have a lock to leave at the Mersey. Martin returned and I pointed the locks out to him. Touchingly, he offered to try to find a hardware store in Liverpool to buy me a lock. I knew we didn't have time to do so; we had to get on the road. I improvised by tying a ribbon that had been placed around a box that held souvenirs for my daughters around the fence rail. As I glanced one more time at the Mersey before leaving I saw my ribbon fluttering in the breeze. I knew it wasn't as permanent as the locks but, then again, nothing is really permanent.

The Mersey is not stagnant; it's always flowing, moving forward, and not looking back at its source nor too far ahead. I sit with it where it meets me-in the present. Leonardo daVinci captured the essence of "now" time in dialoguing with rivers when he wrote, "In rivers, the water that you touch is the last of what has passed and the first of that which comes; so with present time." The Mersey shows me that while change is inevitable and quite natural, transformation is optional. How I meet change in my everyday life defines me. I am learning to not resist change by wanting to hold onto the past or fearing the future. The river shows me that while moving forward, I can break down what appear to be obstacles much like water slowly erodes rock over time. The Mersey also tells me to adapt more; to not bottle myself up with what I feel *should* be the way. Instead, it tells me to handle challenges by finding a way around them in a more delicate way but with forward motion, like the river flows around the buoys that bob in its path.

The Mersey is so far from my "real" life in New Jersey where I live and work, where my life and family are. But I feel more at home on the Mersey in Liverpool than almost anywhere else. I sense that the river and I have a past together, as if it is an old friend with whom I've reconnected. Standing on the walkway above the river, listening to the sounds of the gulls flying overhead, watching the ferry traveling up and down, I am soothed. When not in England, I travel to the Mersey in spirit during times of distress, doubt, and fear. I seek out the river in my

Serendipity

mind when I need peace or want to remember the pure joy of standing beside it.

Like all rivers, the Mersey is always moving. The Mersey shows me that it's important to drop below the surface during turbulent times, to seek out the calm and peace that exists within my soul. It reminds me that my spirit, despite all the turbulence of daily life, is calm by its very nature. It's the human-driven ego that is the part of me that becomes agitated, stirred up, blocked from flowing by forces from both outside of myself and also from those that come from within, namely my thoughts.

I have become one with the Mersey. It tells me to flow through life, to not resist or attempt to swim against the current. The river does not doubt where it's going and it tells me to do the same; to trust where I'm being led, to follow my path.

Souvenirs:

Photograph of the ferry crossing the Mersey.
Tea towel of the ferry.
Two small lithographs of the ferry, one at dawn, one at twilight.
A mug with an image of the ferry.

CHAPTER 5
TWO SMALL SPACES

...You can learn how to be you in time. It's easy. All you need is love.

John Lennon and Paul McCartney

A bedroom and a front parlor-two small spaces that are modest by any definition-small spaces that grew the talents of two men.

I left the hotel in Liverpool cool as a cucumber. Martin and I passed the Beatles Story, an attraction outside of which a group of Japanese tourists were singing in a circle to "Yellow Submarine." Other tourists, clad in an array of Beatles T-shirts, were disembarking from a coach bus. I was trying my best to hide

Serendipity

that today I was really one of *them*, fans who flock to Liverpool to experience the Beatles. As we boarded the large tour bus emblazoned with the words "The Magical Mystery Tour" on its side, my cover and my cool were blown. The trip was going to take us to all the locations associated with the Beatles, including Penny Lane and Strawberry Field. When in Liverpool... well, I *had* to do the tour. There's really no escaping the Beatles in Liverpool or their huge influence around the world that began in these blue-collar streets. Don't get me wrong, I like the Beatles. But I wasn't fanatical and I certainly didn't want to appear that way as I made my way to my seat on the bus.

The bus started its loud engine, the doors closed and, in typical schlocky tourist fashion, the song "Penny Lane" played through the speakers as we headed toward the Penny Lane of Beatles lore. Our driver entered the roundabout mentioned in the song, in the middle of which there actually is a (bus) shelter. We saw the fire station where the fireman kept his engines clean, the barbershop where another customer was shaved, and the bank where apparently the banker never wore a mac in the pouring rain.

We exited the bus to take our photos at the Penny Lane street marker. I hated being seen as a tourist. But I noticed that the residents didn't even glance at the group of us congregating at the street sign, nor at the interloper of a tour bus. Along the lane on this warm afternoon, kids, still wearing their school uniforms, ran into a sweet shop while others waited at the bus stop.

The next stop was Strawberry Field, formerly a Salvation Army home for children that was a short distance from Penny Lane. The bus began to make a wide turn onto a narrow, tree-lined street. Some of my fellow passengers gasped, doubting the skill of the bus driver. A few actually leaned to the right in a visceral attempt to help guide the bus around the turn. I felt a sudden kinship with the driver as I remembered a similar attempt at trying to fit into a tight spot that very morning. My body, having been fed a steady diet of English pub food, (everything brown and fried), had grown a bit too large for jeans that had fit only a week ago when I was still in New Jersey. Undeterred, I had laid across the bed and squeezed into them. Mission accomplished, for both me and for the bus driver who navigated the turn and came to a stop. Turning off the engine, the bus seemed to let out a sigh much as I had done that morning as I zipped up my jeans. Martin and I disembarked and walked to the closed, ornate red wrought-iron gates marking the entrance to Strawberry Field. Graffiti, mostly in homage to the Beatles, covered the gate's stone pillars. It was actually thrilling to be standing at the very place that surely every one of us had sung about one time or another. Was I letting down my guard and on my way to becoming a full-fledged tourist? As much as I tried to resist the excitement, this was beginning to feel dead cool.

While we did only a drive-by of the street where Ringo Starr's childhood home was located, we were able to exit the bus at the home in which George Harrison was born. It is a tiny brick row house, described as a "two-up, two-down," meaning there are two rooms on the first floor and two on the second. The house lacked an indoor bathroom when George lived there. Then it was on to Paul McCartney's childhood home on Forthlin Road. The streets in this neighborhood were wider, the houses seemed newer in construction, and there were small, well-tended gardens in the front yards. There was nothing, though, to differentiate Paul's house from the others, all in their cookie-cutter, brick-fronted style except, that is, for the large crowd standing in front of #20. Exiting the bus, I took the requisite photos in front of the house and at the street sign before walking to the red postbox at end of the street to mail a postcard to my brother and nephews.

Herded back onto the bus, we headed to John Lennon's childhood home. This house was the largest of the four, and unlike the others, was semi-detached. It even had a name, Mendips. In the introduction to a National Trust publication on the home, John's wife, Yoko Ono, wrote, "Liverpool meant a great deal to John. He was always talking about Liverpool, his hometown. It all started in Mendips, his childhood home." When built, the fence surrounding this house was obviously not intended to keep out music fans. But keep us out it did, as we craned our necks in unison in an attempt to see into the backyard that at one time backed onto Strawberry Field. We took our photos against the gate of the house and returned to the bus for the final stop at Mathew Street and the Cavern Club, where the Beatles played some of their early gigs.

Martin and I were visiting Liverpool during one of our annual two-week (or fortnight, as Martin says) vacations to England to see his family. I use this vacation time to not only reconnect with my English family but to also experience Martin's homeland with him as my guide. For fifty weeks of the year Martin is surrounded by my family, but for this brief time our roles are reversed and I participate in activities with his family. I also use this time to take a breather from my everyday roles in the United States and focus completely on myself. I have the time to plug into myself on a much deeper level than I allow myself to do when I am back home. In New Jersey I tend to lose myself in different roles and responsibilities. All too often I stretch myself thin while tending to everyone else's needs. Come time for my August trip to England, my internal home fire has

Serendipity

been reduced to a few smoldering embers. I have neglected the care and feeding of my own heart and soul while running around wearing too many hats and juggling too many plates, inserting myself into situations where I haven't been invited, morphing into the supreme rescuer.

Truthfully, I didn't know how to focus on myself. I was uncomfortable being with me, sitting quietly and hearing that tiny voice that had been trying to get my attention all year, the voice I hushed up with a dismissive wave of my hand because I believed that something or someone always took precedent. I used those annual two weeks in England to reconnect with myself. Only fourteen days, but at least it was a start, up from previous years in which I spent zero days focused on me.

The trips to England gave me time to sit by the door to my soul and gaze at the wonderful world that awaited me once I dared to cross the threshold and walk through. I was beginning to feel small shifts in my attitude that told me I could live a soul-centered life and follow my own unique calling while remaining a mother, a daughter, a wife, a member of my family and my community. Every year while in England I planted seeds of self-love and self-care, vowing to remember to feed and water them when I returned home. I tried to shield those tiny seeds from the harsh winds of critical self-talk that told me that I could never make shifts in my life, that I was too old, that I was selfish, and that I was crazy for trying to change. I was a new and reluctant gardener, so to speak, but I had the desire to make my life bloom. I began to understand that it need not be all work. I could have fun while finally permitting my soul to come forward and thrive in my everyday life. The trip to Liverpool and the Magical Mystery Tour were fun things that I rarely permitted myself the time and money to do.

Martin and I returned to our hotel after the bus tour. I was sorting through the Beatles souvenirs that I had purchased – mugs of Penny Lane, sweatshirts, postcards, tea towels, and key chains. Folding a Cavern Club sweat shirt, I turned to Martin. "Did you have fun today?"

"Yeah, of course. It was so cool to visit those places that the Beatles wrote about. I just wished we could have stopped at the church graveyard where the tour guide told us that there's a tombstone for an Eleanor Rigby."

"Well, I was thinking, maybe tomorrow we could take another tour. I saw one that was sponsored by the National Trust where we could actually enter the homes of John and Paul."

"Wait a minute, Anne! *You* want to go on another guided tour? I thought you hated that kind of stuff."

"Well, normally I do. But I really want to go into the houses. How about it?"

Serendipity

Limited to a handful of people a day, this tour fills quickly. We lucked out and were able to secure tickets for the next day. Bright and early the following morning, we boarded a mini-van with three other couples. I was happily wearing the label of a Beatles tourist now. The driver told us that Bob Dylan had recently taken the tour when he was in town for a concert, sitting in the van just like everyone else. What's cool enough for Dylan is cool enough for me.

The van dropped us off in front of Paul's home. Fans from the other Beatles tours stood outside milling about, taking photos just as Martin and I had done the day before. Today, however, we would actually walk through the front door that Paul (and John) crossed as they made their way home from school to begin writing and rehearsing. Since John's aunt didn't like the two hanging out at her house, the boys would spend the afternoons composing at Paul's home. Over one hundred songs had been written in this house, including "I'll Follow the Sun" and "Yesterday." (Even though the McCartney house belongs to the National Trust, it is not eligible for a commemorative plaque until Paul has been dead for 20 years or until a century has passed since his birth.)

Upon entering the house, the caretaker (who bore an uncanny resemblance to Paul) took our purses, backpacks, cell phones, and cameras. He stayed with us the entire time, moving the group through the house. We were first directed to a small parlor to the left of the front door that had two armchairs and a tiny table in front of a small fireplace. An upright piano was placed against the wall. It was a cheery space filled with sunlight courtesy of a large picture window. Black-and-white photographs taken by Paul's brother when the family lived there hung on the walls in the spots where the photographs were taken. In this front room hung a photograph of the young Lennon and McCartney sitting together near the fireplace, huddled over their guitars; a sheet of paper with the lyrics to "I Saw Her Standing There" lay on the table between them. Music was the invisible furniture that filled the room. I felt as if I was witnessing the creation of this incredible sound, with the boys still present not only through the photographs but through the sheer energy of the space. I could almost hear their voices as they noisily entered the house, making jokes and grabbing a snack before settling down to work.

The tour then moved into a tiny kitchen. A photo of John and Paul making tea hung near the stove. A washing machine shared space in the kitchen and above it hung a photo of Paul unloading laundry. I stood in Paul's upstairs bedroom, a room in which I'm certain thousands of girls on either side of the "pond" dreamed of visiting. Back downstairs, the

Serendipity

tour continued in the tiny backyard where the caretaker directed our attention to a nondescript drainpipe; seemingly unimportant until he pulled out a photo of the boys posing on the very spot. Tour concluded, we were ushered to the front door.

I glanced into the front parlor. This was the room where everything happened. I could practically hear the voices, the laughter, the music, because this was where "Lennon and McCartney" was born. I paused before stepping one more time into the unpretentious room with modest furniture. The energy of the small parlor drew me in. There was a sense of happiness and of nurturing, comfortable and comforting. I wanted to sit in the chair by the fireplace and visit with the family, and strangely, felt welcomed to do so. It was an inviting space; the heart of the home where legend began and where, oddly enough, I felt like part of the family.

"Are you ready?" Martin asked, poking his head into the room where I lingered.

I was the last one in the house and I was apparently holding up the tour.

"Yeah, I'm coming," I said.

Turning to leave the room, I paused one more time to fill my heart with the dreams that began in this room. Exiting, I instinctively reached out and held the doorknob. The other tourists had already piled in the van and were excitedly chatting about the tour. I sat quietly not wanting to lose the feelings and visions that washed over me.

It wasn't far to John's house. A plaque on the house noted that it had been donated to the National Trust by Yoko Ono. John lived in this house with this aunt and uncle because they were able to provide a more stable upbringing than was John's mother. He remained at the house after his mother died from injuries after being hit by a car. After the unexpected death of John's uncle, his Aunt Mimi had to take on boarders to maintain the residence. This house had a less homey feel than Paul's home. It felt like a boarding house where people resided but didn't live together as a family. While well-maintained, I got the feeling that Mimi was keeping up appearances, running a business rather than making a home.

While still required to turn over our possessions, here we were allowed to tour the house at our leisure, unchaperoned. I walked through the kitchen, dining room, and small front parlor. I found myself drawn to places that did not seem to interest the group, places where I could be alone to experience the energy of the space. I was intrigued by the vestibule, the enclosed entryway at the front of the house. Sunlight streamed through the red roses in the stained-glass panels. There were photographs of a young John standing in the exact spot where I stood. I was glad that no one else on the tour bothered to enter this space even though it was apparently where Mimi would send the boys to practice when she did permit them into the home. A tiny area, the space would have been made even tighter with a few boys and their instruments. It wasn't soundproof, either, so I'm sure their voices and music carried throughout the house, likely getting them into trouble, if not booted out completely sooner rather than later.

One of the others from the group walked by, threatening to invade this area that I had temporarily claimed as my own. Wearing a Beatles sweatshirt, the woman quizzically peered at me through the glass, wanting to be sure she hadn't missed anything of note. Finding nothing, she shrugged her shoulders and walked off. *Good*, I thought, *two would have been a crowd*. The others on the tour were leafing through memorabilia in the dining room; photos, letters, report cards. They then moved upstairs to the bedrooms and then back downstairs to talk to the caretaker and wander the backyard.

But something had shifted for me. I was no longer moving through these houses as a Beatles fan. The trip was changing from a tourist destination to a pilgrimage. I remembered hearing about families who use psychics in investigations of missing relatives. The psychics often ask to hold something that belonged to the missing person, believing that objects can hold the energy of the person who possessed it. The process, called psychometry, revolves around the belief that objects owned by someone hold imprints of emotions, sounds, and images. I was *feeling* the energy of these spaces and was inexplicably drawn to certain areas of the two homes, to the places where John and Paul seemed to have spent a large part of their time. There was a deepening in my connection to two souls who, despite humble starts in life, had accomplished so much because they dared to live their dreams and followed their inner calling.

I waited until everyone had left the second floor so that I could enter John's bedroom alone. It had a different vibe from Paul's bedroom. It felt like a sad room, the room of a lonely, restless boy. This was John's only personal space in the house that he shared with the boarders. It had the feeling of being a space that was penning John in, a room from which he wanted to escape; it felt claustrophobic. It was small room in the front of the house. A twin bed with a simple brown headboard was wedged between the wall and the door. A brown desk was placed under the large window that had the same red rose stained-glass patterns as those in the vestibule. Looking out the window, I could look down the street to the spot where John's mother was fatally hit by a car. It must have been heart-wrenching for John to have had to walk by there every day.

Serendipity

For a brief time, I was the only person in the world who was standing in John's childhood bedroom, the room he returned to the evening he learned that his mother had succumbed to her injuries. I looked up at the ceiling that John would have looked at while lying on his bed. What fears or dreams did the room hold? I ran my hand along the bedroom's light switch and started to leave. Pausing with my hand on the doorknob, I felt a connection to John by holding the same object that he touched every day. I could feel his spirit through this most common of objects. It was an energy that was not defensive. I was able to meet John on his turf in the most unguarded of spaces, a childhood bedroom. I became disengaged from John by the voice of the caretaker as he began to gather up the group. Martin called upstairs for me. I touched the doorknob one last time and bid John farewell and peace.

From the two small spaces of the front room of Paul's house and John's bedroom a realization grew in me that we are all capable of achieving great things by having the fortitude to follow our heart's desire, the courage to not only dream but to act on those dreams. It doesn't matter where we are born, how we grew up, what opportunities were presented, or what hardships we faced, we all come to this earth with a gift to share. I thought about the many times I had harbored small thoughts, safe thoughts and, worst of all, settled for less in my life. I used to believe that other people could do great things because, well, they had greatness. But those two small spaces in the childhood homes of John Lennon and Paul McCartney showed me that nothing was further from the truth. In those small spaces that I was privileged to briefly inhabit, I was wrapped in a cocoon of empowerment, of hope, of faith in myself. It had nothing to do with the material success and international fame achieved by John and Paul. It was the symbol they became to me of not settling for what's safe, but always reaching for what is my right, to fully step into life, to live an authentic life, to heed my soul calling. Visiting those spaces in Liverpool caused me to remember that, while a cocoon protects and nurtures, it also fosters growth and transformation, until eventually something amazing emerges.

Souvenirs:

Books of the National Trust house tour.
Mugs from Cavern Club and Penny Lane.
Beatles leather bookmark.
Cavern Club sweatshirt.
Tea towels of Beatles sites.
Way too many Beatles-related Christmas presents.

CHAPTER 6
GLASTONBURY

And so perhaps, the truth winds somewhere between the road to Glastonbury, Isle of the Priests, and the road to Avalon, lost forever in the mists of the Summer Sea.

The Mists of Avalon, Marion Zimmer Bradley

I didn't set out to Glastonbury for the purpose of making a pilgrimage, but a pilgrimage it became; my serendipity pilgrimage. I had never heard of Glastonbury, a small town in Somerset, southwest

England, until Martin mentioned it as a possible side trip during our summer visit to his family. I didn't know about its annual music festival that had featured musicians like Bruce Springsteen, the Rolling Stones, and the Who. I knew nothing of its connection to King Arthur, the Holy Grail, fairies, and ley lines. Martin and I were having breakfast at the tiny kitchen table in his parents' house, deciding where to go for a long weekend. Laundry hung from a wooden rack above our heads. Well, it was mostly my laundry, and more specifically, my panties, or knickers, as Martin referred to them. When the weather was inclement, my mother-in-law hung the laundry to dry on a ceiling rack, an old wooden contraption suspended over the kitchen that was rigged in place by means of a pulley system. Martin's family walked under the rack on their way to the stove, sink, and tea kettle. No one except me seemed to notice the overhead peep show, meals eaten under a canopy sponsored by Victoria's Secret.

Martin put a spoon in his breakfast cereal of Weetabix and then paused. "I think we should go to Glastonbury for the weekend, Anne. It's a magical place. There are so many myths and stories surrounding the town. Some people think that Glastonbury was where Avalon was located. And you're so into crystals and energy fields that I know you're going to love the New Age feeling that Glastonbury is known

Serendipity

for. It's not close but it's definitely worth the trip. What do you think?"

Wow. Glastonbury sounded like a place that combined a lot of my interests-history, alternative healing, and legends. "I'm in!"

Decision made, Martin booked us into the George Hotel and Pilgrims' Inn, built in the 1400s to accommodate pilgrims traveling to Glastonbury Abbey. As we packed, Martin filled me in a little more on Glastonbury. He spoke of Glastonbury's connection to King Arthur and Queen Guinevere, whose tombs were supposedly uncovered there in the 12th century by the monks at Glastonbury Abbey. This bolstered the belief that the town was once the island of Avalon, the place where King Arthur was taken to recover from battle wounds. Supporting the claim is the fact that at one time Glastonbury was surrounded by marshland, essentially making it an island. For ages Glastonbury has also been known a center of goddess worship, with Morgan le Fay having a prominent role. And apparently, the town even has a connection to Jesus. According to some, Joseph of Arimathea visited Glastonbury with an adolescent Jesus and then returned years after the crucifixion of Jesus with the Holy Grail which he buried in Glastonbury.

As I threw a few sweaters into my overnight bag, Martin transitioned to Glastonbury's reputation as a

New Age gathering place with claims of the healing power of its natural energy. "Some believe that the planet is encircled by highways of energy called ley lines," he explained. "And Glastonbury is considered to be one site where the ley lines converge, creating a vortex of positive energy. A lot of people travel to Glastonbury to experience this energy and to participate in all sorts of New Age rituals and treatments. And," he continued, "the area surrounding the town supposedly forms a landscape zodiac, a map of the stars formed by streams, ancient roads, and other types of markers like hedgerows and stone walls. This is your kind of place, Anne. You're going to love it," he promised as he backed the rental car out of his parents' driveway.

How come I'd never heard of Glastonbury? I wondered, as we began our journey south. I settled in for the four-hour drive. Martin was never one for conversation while he was driving and this was especially so when we were in England where he had to drive on the opposite side of the car on the opposite side of the road. He put on a CD as I looked out the window. I was really excited about going to Glastonbury, but I was also bit homesick for my daughters and feeling more than a little guilty at taking a two-week vacation without them. Was I a selfish mother? My mind needed little prompting to push aside Martin's stories of Glastonbury and replace them with a to-do

Serendipity

list for self-improvement. As the cars whizzed by on the highway, I began a mental inventory of things I had done "wrong," and of things I could have done better over the past few years. Then, in true self-loving fashion, I broadened the period of inventory to include my entire life. How could I switch from fun to self-attack so quickly? It was easy; I had practiced it all my life. And you know what they say: you get good at what you practice.

A few months earlier, I had begun to see an acupuncturist for knee pain because I wanted to avoid medication. Never having been to one before, I assumed that she would stick a lot of needles in the area around my knee. I laid on the table and she began to insert the thin needles in my chest. I was surprised when said that she was going to concentrate a lot of the initial session on my heart chakra, which seemed to be in need "opening." Chakras, from the Sanskrit for turning wheel, are considered to be the seven centers of energy in our bodies. Starting at the base of the spine and extending up to the crown of the head, each chakra is associated with certain emotions, colors, and parts of the body. When a chakra is balanced, all is well, and the energy or *chi*, is able to flow freely through the body, resulting in a sense of physical and emotional well-being. When a chakra has been blocked by an emotional upset like conflict or loss, the flow of energy is slowed or stopped, manifesting in physical or emotional problems.

The acupuncturist explained that the heart chakra controls our ability to give and receive love. I prided myself on my ability to give love to others, but I really did have a very hard time showing love to myself and even receiving love from others. When people paid attention to me in loving ways I often felt very uncomfortable, not worthy of the attention on some deep level. She cautioned me against falling into this martyr syndrome where I gave too much of myself to others while denying myself a place in my own life. The resulting emotions of anger and resentment were toxic to the body, she warned. Gently inserting the thin needles as she spoke, she explained that the heart chakra is the center chakra and that a blockage there could cause one or more of the other chakras to become unbalanced. She worked on my heart chakra for the subsequent visits while I continued to work on self-love.

Riding in the car to Glastonbury, I realized that I was mentally punishing myself for having fun. I looked over at Martin. He was laughing to a Bonzo Dog Band CD that he had purchased at Meadowhall in Sheffield. I sighed and returned to looking out the car window, making a promise to be more kind to myself. I began compiling a list of ways that I had done my best, of ways that I was a good mother, or daughter, or friend. But the list focused on what I had done for others. Where was I in my own life? I had a life-long pattern of putting the needs of others before my own and had only recently begun to shift that way of thinking to create a life that was more self-centered. Not in a selfish way, not in a greedy way, but in a more loving and accepting way toward myself.

Radical self-care, as it's called in some circles, includes carving out time for activities such as forgiving yourself, doing what you love, and taking care of your body through healthy eating, resting, and exercising. For me it should have been labeled "self-preservation" at this point because I had so neglected myself over the years. I'd find myself doing everything that was asked of me even if I didn't have the time or inclination to do it and, worst of all, doing things for others that *weren't* even asked of me because I thought it was my duty to be all things to all people. The resulting guilt (of feeling I didn't do enough) and anger (from feeling I did too much) threatened to consume me. Self-love and self-acceptance were going to help me to open my heart chakra and assist with bringing my soul, mind, and body into alignment. Once I became whole and healthy I could then help others in a healthier manner. That's how it works: you can't give what you don't have. I needed to do for myself before I could do for others.

I had been learning all of this from the books that the acupuncturist recommended. But now I had to take the words from the books and put them to action in my life.

Martin's voice snapped me back to the drive. We seemed to have suddenly come upon a plain where livestock grazed but, then again, I hadn't been paying attention to the drive. Ahead, a hill encircled by what appeared to be terraces carved into its side appeared in the middle of the flat, green landscape. It was capped by what looked to be a church. Glastonbury lay before us, atmospherically shrouded in mist.

"That's the Tor," Martin said, nodding in the direction of the hill.

"The what?"

"The Tor. It's thought to be the entrance to the land of the fairies and also possibly the site where the Holy Grail is buried. We'll climb it either today or tomorrow. But for now keep your eyes open for High Street. Let's park the car and find the inn." This town promised to be different from the other towns in England that I had visited. Jesus, Avalon, the Holy Grail, ley lines, the Tor, and fairies – I wasn't in New Jersey anymore.

We parked in the car lot behind the George Hotel and Pilgrims' Inn, a three-story stone building with arched windows, the old glass wavy and

Serendipity

distorted. As pilgrims did over six hundred years earlier, we crossed the low threshold and checked in. The hotel's pub had some afternoon lingerers who barely raised their heads as we entered. The interior was dark and musty. We were pointed in the direction of our room which was very small, with space only for a bed and dresser. The low wood-beamed ceiling and tiny doorway brought to mind how much smaller people were in the 15th century. We dropped our bags, had a quick bite to eat in the pub, and then stepped out into the grey day. Walking along the narrow streets, we looked into shop windows that offered stones and crystals of all shapes and sizes- amethyst, tourmaline, and citrine. I bought a small, heart-shaped rose quartz for each of my daughters. Bookstores displayed titles on subjects like meditation and the use of color therapy for healing. Handwritten signs taped on windows advertised a menu of alternative healing offerings, including past life regression, Reiki, and sound therapy.

Turning a corner, we came upon the remnants of Glastonbury Abbey, silent testimony to the town's religious importance in medieval times. Martin, my walking encyclopedia noted that before being destroyed on the orders of Henry VIII, Glastonbury Abbey was once second only to Westminster Abbey in terms of its wealth. The abbey was built on the site of an Anglo-Saxon church, which seems to not be that uncommon. I'd read that over the ages people were drawn to what could only be termed a sacred site and that as one religion lost power, another group of people built their own religious structures on the same site. Such places are sometimes called "thin" places, where the veil between the seen and unseen is thought to be more permeable. The midday sky was beginning to darken as we entered the abbey grounds. The abbey looked like an unfinished three-dimensional jigsaw puzzle: fragments of walls devoid of stained glass and doors, vegetation filling spaces once occupied by worshippers. Three large pieces of the abbey's nave and transept survive, as does the now roofless Lady Chapel that was dedicated to the Virgin Mary.

Writings as early as 633 contain information that an ancient church was built on the site of Glastonbury Abbey. It had one of the earliest chapels north of Italy to be dedicated to the Virgin Mary. There are also accounts that an ancient statue of Mary survived a fire that destroyed the chapel. When Glastonbury Abbey was built, the Lady Chapel dedicated to Mary, was built on the site of this ancient chapel. The statue of Mary was housed there and became the focus of a pilgrimage. There was even a connection between the Virgin Mary and King Arthur. A 12th century account by Gerald of Wales noted King Arthur's devotion to the Virgin Mary. There is speculation that the mortally wounded Arthur was taken to Avalon to be near the Lady Chapel.

We left the abbey to travel to the Tor. By the time we reached the Tor it had begun to drizzle. The soft green hill was encircled with subtle ridges. A narrow stone and dirt footpath ran straight up one side leading to what looked like the remnants of a small church at its summit. I made a valiant attempt to begin the walk up but the slick, muddy walkway, combined with my fear of heights, made me do an about-face. I waved Martin on and walked to the base to wait for him. People milled around me, each having their own personal experience with the Tor. A man of around thirty with dreadlocks was beating on a small wooden drum. A woman dressed in a multi-colored skirt and flowing blouse danced to the drum's beats, her arms gracefully moving in circles around her head. A couple sat cross-legged on the ground, arms outstretched to the sky.

The Tor was more than a tourist destination. People were interacting with the site itself. So I didn't feel self-conscious at all as I stood at its base and planted my feet into the muddy soil. A woman in black yoga pants and a red sweater approached me. "Be careful not to fall asleep at the Tor. You might be whisked away by the fairies," she cautioned. Was she joking? "It's especially important not to do so on May Day or Midsummer because that's when the gates to fairy land open." She was serious. I thanked her for the warnings.

Taking my chances with the fairies, I closed my eyes, envisioning drawing the earth's grounding energy upward through my body. I then did the reverse, pulling the energy from the sky above, down through my body and back into the earth, making a continuous loop of energy, the infinity symbol. I pictured something akin to an electrical current traveling through my chakras, each one spinning its own unique color. I inhaled slowly, feeling the breath expand in my chest before exhaling equally as slowly. The flow of the earth's energy, though, seemed to be a little blocked as it approached my heart chakra, so I mentally gave my heart a little massage, softening it with some gentle kneading. I had experience doing this exercise through the guided meditations that often ended my yoga classes in New Jersey as we lay in *savasana*, the final pose. Sometimes referred to as "corpse pose," it was my favorite pose because I got to lay on the mat with a blanket on, my eyes covered with a lavender-scented eye pillow.

"Hello, Anne. Are you there?"

I had been so focused that I hadn't heard Martin's approach.

"I wish you had been able to make the climb. The views from the top of the Tor were spectacular! A man was able to point out to me the Welsh mountains in the distance."

"Well, you know me and my fear of heights. Besides, I had my own encounter with the Tor-but at base level-my favorite level."

Martin had been exposed to my thoughts on energy, chakras, and angels since we had begun dating a few years earlier. A skeptic, he was at least open to hearing my experiences, such as my energy work done at the Tor that day, which we discussed on our way back to the inn. I wasn't looking to convert him, but it was important to be able to share with him the things that were meaningful to me. He listened, and that's all that I was asking for. I knew that he supported my beliefs, though. He was the one, after all, who recommended the trip to Glastonbury because he knew I would want to experience this extraordinary place.

After dinner we took another walk to the abbey as the sun was setting. The orange sky shone through the stone frames that had once held the abbey's windows, creating a natural replacement to the lost stained glass. Glastonbury's atmosphere was charged; there was an otherworldly feeling to the town. It was something I felt, although I couldn't explain it. It was as if different periods of time continued to exist simultaneously. Because of that, I never felt alone, even when I walked by myself the following evening to Mass at the Church of Our Lady of Saint Mary. I felt as if I was joined on the walk by ghosts of the past, the hooded monks of the abbey, the dust-covered pilgrims making their way through the town, and the ethereal fairies who lived below the Tor. Although Martin had initially decided to stay back at the inn, toward the end of Mass he slipped into my pew to accompany me back to the inn.

On the day we were checking out, Martin struck up a conversation with the desk clerk.

"Does anyone ever see any ghosts here?"

"Well, actually, you and your wife stayed in the room where the most sightings occur. People repeatedly mention seeing a monk walk quickly across the room with his head down."

Thin veil.

I walked outside as Martin finished paying the bill and began speaking with a woman standing on the sidewalk. She told me she practiced Reiki. As we discussed the benefits of alternative healing, she said that Glastonbury's location is thought to be the heart chakra of the planet. Chills ran up my arms as I remembered the heart-shaped rose quartz stones I had purchased for the girls and all the work I did with my heart chakra at the Tor.

This visit transformed into a pilgrimage to a site that has its power in the earth. This land has had a magnetic draw for thousands of years attracting "pagans," early Christians, medieval pilgrims, and those interested in its connections to the Druid, Arthurian, and Celtic legends, and the Divine Feminine. *Nothing is coincidence*, I thought, including how Martin felt drawn to take me to Glastonbury at a time when I was in need of some heart-opening. I had never before experienced the raw power of the Earth for healing that I had found in Glastonbury. The natural energy was abundant, loving, and nourishing, and flowed into my slowly expanding heart.

Souvenirs:

A wooden carving of the Green Man, a deity representing rebirth, who wears a mask of foliage.
A horse brass of Glastonbury Abbey.
Bookmark of Glastonbury.
Tea towel of Glastonbury.
Heart-shaped rose quartz stones for my daughters.

CHAPTER 7
ROME: DREAMS REALIZED

For us to go to Italy and to penetrate into Italy is like a most fascinating act of self-discovery.... Strange and wonderful chords awake in us, and vibrate again after many hundreds of years of complete forgetfulness.

Sea and Sardinia, D.H. Lawrence

I wanted to savor the moment at the very real risk of being overrun by fellow passengers rushing from the plane's walkway to the terminal of the Leonardo DaVinci International Airport. I tried to walk slowly, wanting to remember the exact moment when I first stepped onto Italian soil-well, the blue airport carpet to be technical-in Fiumicino, a short distance from Rome. I had arrived, fulfilling my dream. My trip to Italy was the geographical reverse of that made by my immigrant great-grandparents and my grandfather, Albert. Despite the difference in the directions traveled, we shared a dream of finding something in a foreign land that had eluded us at home. My ancestors had embarked on their voyages searching for better opportunities for jobs, an improved standard of living, and a stable place to raise their growing families. I came to Italy in the hope of finding a significant someone with whom I had lost contact-myself.

My great-grandparents tried as best they could to recreate their Italian provinces of Benevento and Corigliano in the narrow streets of South Philadelphia. While lacking the expansive views and hilltop vistas of their villages, their adopted city offered far-reaching prospects. Their neighborhood was little more than a slum when they arrived in the early 20th century. Today, it is a gentrified 21st century neighborhood that has ironically been renamed Belle Vista, or beautiful view, by the realtors.

My grandfather, Umberto Aita, who Americanized his name to Albert in the 1930s when he became an American citizen, told stories of his voyage to Philadelphia in 1915 that captivated me as a child. "We were told that the streets in America were paved with gold," he'd remember as I sat on the floor near his reclining chair. He was a thin man with warm brown eyes and a pencil mustache. I'd search his face for signs of disappointment.

How sad they must have felt, I thought, when, after all that time at sea, they found the streets were only made of bricks and asphalt. I felt so sorry for my grandfather.

But his eyes would light up as he continued. "And they were, *figlia di papa*! There were so many riches in this new land."

Growing up I loved listening to the stories told of immigrant great-grandparents raising large families of ten and twelve children in the tiny row houses of South Philadelphia. Each family had one formal black-and-white family portrait of mostly unsmiling faces of people who looked much older than their years, the patriarch standing with his hand stiffly resting on the shoulder of the seated matriarch. These photographs now hang in my parents' house; the eyes of my ancestors continue to look out at me through the generations that separate us, our gazes locking.

These families faced hardships that I can't fathom, such as the deaths of children from illnesses

Serendipity

that today generally aren't fatal. Photographs were a luxury to these very poor people, reserved for special occasions such as weddings. Children were generally not photographed-except in death. There are sepia-toned death portraits of two of the children of my great-grandmother, Maria Antonia Tomaselli. In one image, the grief-stricken mother, herself a child of only sixteen, holds her firstborn, Amelia. Rather than looking at the child in her arms, Maria stares into the distance. I imagine that it was too heartbreaking for her to look upon the one-year-old child dressed in a lace outfit who lay stiffly in her arms. The child is the size of a large doll; her tiny face is framed with long brown curls. In another photograph, eleven-year-old Pasquelina rests in a coffin in the family's parlor covered in white satin blankets. Reflective of the fashion of 1910, her long hair is held in place with a large white bow that overwhelms her small face. Her mouth is slightly open as if caught in mid-whisper. Death had once again visited the family with another child-sized coffin, candelabra, and sprays of condolences flowers taking up residence in the tiny home.

For these immigrants, the concept of family extended to neighbors, many of whom came from the same villages in Italy. When one family experienced a hardship, the other neighbors pitched in. My great-grandparents, Maria Antonia and Michael

Tomaselli, lived in a tiny row house in South Philadelphia with their ten children. The small house had been sectioned into two by the landlord, who wanted to collect multiple rents. The family who resided in the back section of the house had an equally large family. When the mother of the neighboring family died in childbirth, Maria cared for both families, effectively raising sixteen children until homes could be found for the motherless children, including a newborn, whose father was unprepared to care for them.

Life was hard for this first generation in America. My great-grandparents were illiterate, as noted on the census records. The Italian dialect of their province was their first language and they only ever acquired very limited abilities to speak and understand English. They relied on the translation skills of their young children-my grandparents and great-aunts and great-uncles-to help them navigate in their adopted country when they had to interact with non-Italians. I remember hearing them speak in broken English; I imitated their pronunciation of words. I called a family friend Mudalen her whole life as that was how she pronounced her name, only later realizing that her name was Madeline. I still say *mootsadel* instead of mozzarella.

None of my grandparents went to school past the eighth grade because they had to work to help support the family. And work, of course, extended into the summer months when they would take a two-hour trip on a rickety, un-air conditioned bus to the fields of rural southern New Jersey to pick vegetables. (Ironically, I now live in that area; what grows on this land now are stores like Anthropologie.) Everyone pitched in, even the youngest children, who worked alongside their older siblings. My ancestors were poor but generous. "My parents barely had enough food to feed us," my grandmother Rose would often tell me. "But they never turned away a hungry body." (Rose-a lovely name but her mother wanted to name her Ursula after her own mother; the problem was that the midwife didn't know how to spell Ursula, so they named her Rose, which the midwife could spell.)

Much like my young body was fed a steady diet of macaroni and gravy (red sauce), my heart was instilled with the beliefs that you always had enough to share and that hospitality was an expectation; treat guests as *famiglia*. I am proud to have descended from these hard-working people; a stone carver who crafted mausoleums, a street sweeper, a pressman, a seamstress who did piecemeal work from home, and a milkman who delivered from a horse-drawn cart. What the family tried to keep on the low down was that one great-grandfather sometimes worked as a nude model at the Pennsylvania Academy of Fine

Arts. We don't know how it was acquired, but one of Philadelphia's finest Italian restaurants has a large photograph of my great-grandfather posing in a strategically draped sheet. Busted.

It was only after my trip to Italy that I really understood that, however challenging life was in this new land at that time, my immigrant family actually did find America to be the land of opportunity. I understood why my grandfather's story of believing that the streets in America were paved with gold didn't have a disappointing ending. They had found what they were looking for, with each generation achieving a little more than the preceding one. They were strong people, they were risk-takers, they were caring and generous, and they were proud people. I took the advice that I heard Patti Smith give during a commencement speech at the Pratt Institute in 2010: *Your ancestors sing through your blood. Call to them. Their strength through the ages will come into you.* I knew that I had to visit Italy someday.

I had longed to travel to Italy ever since I sat at my Grandpop Albert's knee. Italy was my ancestral home and also relevant to my then-job as a college instructor of Art History and Art Appreciation. Semester after semester, I would lead my students through ancient Rome and Renaissance cities like Venice and Florence via slide presentations. Some semesters I taught seven courses at three community colleges. The day students were usually right out of high school. I'd listen with envy as they'd tell me about senior class trips to Italy. I asked one student to tell the class about his tour of the Sistine Chapel.

"Oh, I didn't go in. I had to pay extra so I decided to pass." It took all of my willpower to not hit him upside the head.

"You traveled all the way to Italy, found your way to Rome and the Sistine Chapel, and you didn't want to pay to see Michelangelo's paintings of the ceiling and the *Last Judgment*? So, you sat outside and ate a piece of pizza?"

Students in my evening classes tended to be of nontraditional college age, a nice way of saying they were over the age of twenty-five. One such student pulled me aside at the end of class one night. She'd just returned from a two-week tour of Italy. "I can't believe that you bring these cities and artists to life for us but you haven't visited Italy. You need to get yourself there and experience the art and architecture first-hand. I thought of you the whole time I was there. You'll be an even better teacher for it. Go," she directed.

I knew she was right. Italy would feed my eyes with its art, architecture, and landscape. It would nourish my body with its food and wine. I hoped it would also nourish my soul, which longed for a reconnection to the Roman Catholic faith in which I was raised but from whose church I had grown disenfranchised. I wanted to proudly return to Italy in gratitude for my ancestors who were born there and, with giant leaps of faith, took the two-week voyage in steerage across the Atlantic Ocean in the hopes of bettering their lives and those of their children and future generations. I knew that I had to get to Italy. But a divorce derailed my travel plans. Having two children to care for and a mortgage to pay, I returned to working a full-time day job as a higher education administrator while continuing to teach three evening Art History classes. Travel to Italy remained a far-off dream to me then, certainly not a priority.

Through divorce I lost not only a husband, but also myself. Although not asked, I willed it upon myself to be everything to my children. The guilt that so often accompanies divorce caused me to think it would be selfish to do things for me. Believing that the failed marriage had ruined their lives, I devoted myself to making sure my daughters were happy and that they felt secure at all times. I didn't understand that I could care for myself and care for them at the same time, that doing one didn't cancel out the other. After the divorce I made a conscious decision to put my life on hold.

Over time, however, something began to shift. The call to travel to Italy began to bubble up from within. Quietly at first, I felt the gentle nudges and reminders of this longing. I'd flip through travel books at the library or look up the plane fare to Rome. I would try to silence the longing, sometimes quite harshly, with a wagging of the proverbial finger. *Italy? Are you kidding? You can't think about that now. You have the girls to take care of and the house to maintain. Maybe in a few decades from now, once you get everything in order.*

But this persistent inner voice, needing to be heard, refused to be silent. The quiet nudges turned into shouting. *I want to go to Italy! Why don't you take the girls with you? Pack up your family and take them on this trip. Bring your girls to Italy to complete the circle begun by your great-grandparents.*

Our annual vacations were always very modest-a ninety-minute trip by car to the Jersey shore, where we'd either rent a house off-season for a long weekend or stay at the home of my sister and her husband. How would I raise funds for three airfares to Italy when the cost of one international ticket seemed prohibitive? I needed a plan to get the girls and me to Italy.

The only way the trip to Italy was even a remote possibility was to begin small-scale saving as a family. We literally began saving our pennies. I'd make all my purchases using only bills, no change. If the purchase was $2.37, for example, I'd hand over $3 and put the 63 cents into a small brown wicker box designated to hold our Italy travel fund. The box drew no attention as it sat under a table in the foyer, but it contained coins from our shopping trips. Every few months the girls looked forward to going to the bank's change-counting machine to see how much we had saved. I opened a separate account for the Italy fund and, amazingly, in ten years we had actually saved enough for our plane tickets.

Emily was then in her final year of high school and Alanna was a sophomore in college. Time seemed to be running out for any travels together. The girls would soon begin to scatter: Emily to college, Alanna to graduate school or the workforce where her vacation time (not to mention finances) would be limited. Soon after she returned to campus to begin her junior year, Alanna emailed me of an opportunity to study abroad in Rome for five weeks over the coming summer. I was determined that Emily and I would join her in Rome at the end of her studies. Alanna signed up for the program, and a month before her departure, she received her *very* full itinerary. Since she was on a shortened term, she would be attending class every single weekday. Her weekends would be filled with field trips to cities like Florence and Siena. The possibility of extending Alanna's stay in Italy to accommodate a visit by Emily and me was not appealing to either one of the girls. Alanna wanted to get back to her part-time job before the start of the fall semester, and Emily needed to get ready for her move to college. I was extremely disappointed, but I also didn't want to force a trip that would be stressful. We decided to postpone our dream trip.

Alanna departed for Rome in late June. And then began the steady stream of emailed photographs and details about her experiences with "gladiators" at the Colosseum, the Tuscan landscape, and the narrow, cobble-stoned streets of Florence. I was experiencing my trip to Italy vicariously, happy for her to have this opportunity to briefly live there. It moved me to see photographs of her in front of the *Gates of Paradise* in Florence and Saint Peter's Basilica in Vatican City. A week into her trip, I received the following email from Alanna (yes, I saved it):

I think you and Emily should come any time after the 15th if it's still possible. This isn't fun without having people that mean something with me to share it with. If it's still an option, I'd love to have you guys here. I'd have plenty of time to spend with you as it turns out.

I began to cry as I read the email. The trip was on. I dialed the travel agent and within 24 hours had booked our flight to Italy, found a hotel run by an order of monks, put in my vacation time at work, and reserved tickets to the Sistine Chapel and the Colosseum. We were set to go. At least I thought we were. Everything had fallen into place so easily. What could go wrong?

A week before we were set to depart, I received a phone call from Emily.

"Mom, I'm so sorry," she sobbed over and over again. "I'm okay but I'm scared. Can you come and get me?"

"Emily," I shouted into the phone, "where are you? What happened?"

"I had an accident. It's bad but I'm okay. I'm so sorry, Mom, the car is ruined."

It was a warm summer evening and I had been sitting on the porch. An hour earlier Emily and her friend jumped in her car and waved good-bye as they set off to buy ice cream. As I stood up to go back into the house my cell phone rang. It was Emily calling about the accident. I reached inside the front door, grabbed my purse and car keys and began to run to the car when the touch of the stones on the driveway caused me to realize that I had forgotten to put on shoes. I don't remember driving to the accident scene. As I turned onto the road where Emily told me she was I saw the flashing lights of police cars, ambulances, and a fire engine in the distance. Thankfully she had called me or I would have thought the worse. She had totaled her car but was lucky to have survived the accident with little more than some bumps, bruises, and cuts from flying

Serendipity

glass. It would be an understatement to say that we were shaken. While Emily was relatively unscathed physically, the emotional scars were another matter. After some x-rays and a few hours of observation, she was released from the emergency room.

We walked out of the hospital just as the sun was rising. I helped her into the car and buckled her seat belt. She reclined the seat and closed her eyes. We were both exhausted. She fell asleep on the ride home. All I could do was shake my head and count my blessings. The trip to Italy hung in the balance, but it didn't matter after what had happened. A few days later the doctor cleared Emily to travel and she decided that she wanted to continue with the trip, looking forward to getting on a plane and leaving behind the trauma of the accident. A week later we sat in the airport waiting to board the flight to Rome and be reunited with Alanna. This was going to be the first time that I would travel out of the country with no one to guide me, and the first time I would travel to a non-English-speaking country. The stars were aligned for this to be a true adventure, just me and my girls.

Emily and I were exhausted when we deplaned in Italy. Unsure of navigating my way to the hotel via public transportation, I had arranged for a driver to meet us at the airport. The initial highway drive to the hotel looked a bit like the New Jersey Turnpike that

I had left behind. (Trust me, only Bruce Springsteen can romanticize the New Jersey Turnpike.) But soon Emily and I were being driven at a fairly high speed through the windy streets of Rome until we arrived at the hotel which was located just outside the walls of Vatican City. Run by an order of monks, it was simple but clean, convenient, and safe. We didn't need more than the two beds, desk, wardrobe, and shower that it provided. Oh yeah, and the crucifix that hung above my bed. The sight of the dome of Saint Peter's Basilica greeted us each time we left the hotel.

That first day we settled in and arranged to meet Alanna for lunch. Emily and I dropped our bags in the room, changed our clothes, freshened up a bit and dashed out the door. The friendly man at the front desk took our room key, hung it on a board behind him, and pointed us in the direction of where we were to meet Alanna. Jet lagged, we passed cafes where patrons lingered at outdoor tables, gelato shops that tempted with a rainbow of offerings behind refrigerated glass cases, and street vendors selling rosary beads and religious statues. Since I really hadn't slept in 24 hours, I felt as if I was walking through a dream-a decades-long dream.

Moving through an underground walkway below the busy street, we exited at Saint Peter's. I stood transfixed. Every Christmas Eve after returning home from our traditional meal of the seven

Serendipity

fishes with the family, the girls and I would watch the Papal Mass from the Vatican on television. And now I was standing at that very site. Pilgrims milled about, some waiting in the line that snaked around Bernini's colonnade, others snapping photos or quietly talking in groups. We had no time to linger because we had to meet Alanna at the Metro. Quickly crossing Saint Peter's Square, we followed the directions of the hotel concierge to the Ottaviano Metro stop. *I can't believe I'm in Rome, I can't believe I'm in Rome, I can't believe I'm in Rome,* I kept thinking as we walked to the Metro stop, sounding like a one-off version of Dorothy in the *Wizard of Oz*. Just as we approached the corner, Alanna emerged from the underground station into the brilliant sunlit day, reminding me of a modern-day Botticelli Venus, only one born from the Metro, not the sea. The girls squealed and ran into each other's arms. Pulling up the rear, I joined my daughters in a group hug. I had fulfilled my dream. The girls and I were in Rome. But this was only the beginning.

We had a nice lunch in a small restaurant that Alanna recommended. She then dropped us off at the Spanish Steps and continued on to her afternoon class. The day's heat was made bearable by our first trip to a gelato stand. Emily and I savored the cold, creamy delicacy while sitting on the crowded steps. About an hour later we walked back to the hotel to shower before meeting Alanna for dinner. Afraid we would fall into a deep sleep and miss our meal, we only allowed ourselves a short nap before setting off again in the direction of the Metro. Alanna took us to dinner at a restaurant near her dorm. The wait staff had come to know her and joked with her on her Italian pronunciations as she ordered for us. "Il conto," she said, requesting the check. The tall, dark, and handsome young waiter refused to hand over the check until she corrected her pronunciation to sound like *eel conto*.

On the walk back to the dorm, Alanna took us to her favorite gelato shop, where we indulged in our second such treat of the day. Emily and I made sure Alanna got safely to the dorm before we set off for the Metro stop, only to find out that it was so late that the buses and Metro had stopped running. Unable to catch a taxi, we walked a few miles back to the hotel, where we collapsed onto our beds.

Over the next couple of days, I guided my girls through the cathedrals and museums, speaking as mom/art history teacher. At the Borghese Gallery we marveled at Bernini's exquisite sculptures, especially that of Apollo and Daphne. Bernini's rendering in marble of Daphne's hair morphing into leaves is an artistic marvel. This jewel of a museum also houses paintings by DaVinci, Caravaggio, and Raphael. Exiting the museum, the girls walked ahead down

Serendipity

a tree-lined path in the Borghese gardens, giggling and catching up.

Emily had requested that we visit Santa Maria della Vittoria so that she could see her favorite work of art, Bernini's *Ecstasy of Saint Teresa*. This 17th-century church is not one of Rome's most noted and so was not one with which the hotel's concierge was familiar. Eventually, he figured out the church's location and directed us to the Repubblica Metro stop. We had to walk a few blocks from the Metro to the church. It was late morning and we quickened our pace because the church was set to close for three hours, beginning at noon. We were temporarily distracted from our mission, though, by the site of lemon trees that lined the sidewalks. Arriving in the nick of time, we sprinted up the steps and quietly entered the cool, darkened church. There were only a few people in the building. The altar was ornate but could not compete for Emily's attention. She moved rapidly to the left side of the altar where the sculpture of Saint Teresa hung. I purposely stood back to watch her approach the sculpture that, until now, she had only been able to admire in books. Her head turned upward and her mouth opened in awe. Without realizing it, she was mimicking the facial expression of the saint in ecstasy. Alanna joined her sister and dropped a coin into a box below the statue, causing the sculpture to be briefly illuminated.

Oh my, I am so blessed, I whispered to myself. The three of us stood looking up at Saint Teresa, her lips sensually parted as the angel pierces her with an arrow. We had witnessed Bernini's mastery of marble many times on this trip, but this sculpture was the culmination, particularly because it was Emily's favorite. We sat for a while in the dimly lit church, I in quiet prayer. As we exited, the Roman sun shone brightly in our eyes as we looked for a place to eat lunch.

The next day we visited the Vatican Museum and the Sistine Chapel. Sitting along a wall in the Sistine Chapel, I quietly described the process of fresco painting and Michelangelo's hidden images on the ceiling and in his painting *The Last Judgment* on the altar wall. The hushed admonition of *silencio* from the Chapel's guards to the tourists periodically pierced the air. Being in the Sistine Chapel certainly did allow me to better appreciate the agonizing work both physically and mentally that Michelangelo endured for four long years while painting the ceiling. My former student was right: experiencing Italy was greatly deepening my appreciation of the art and architecture. But more importantly, it was also deepening my appreciation of me, because this was more than a nine-day art history tour of Italy; it was evidence of my ability to fulfill a dream.

Alanna, who had not been to Mass in years, asked that Emily and I meet her at Saint Peter's to attend

Serendipity

services on our only Sunday in Rome. I learned long ago not to express too much happiness at something good that one of my daughters is doing, because then whatever it is will soon cease, and quickly. I contained my joy on this one, playing it cool saying, "Sure, Emily and I will be there at 11:30."

"Okay, but remember, Mom, you and Emily have to dress conservatively in order to enter. See you then." Alanna reminding us to dress conservatively? Wonder of wonders.

Mass, said in Italian, was celebrated in an intimate spot behind the basilica's main altar, which was flanked by Bernini's towering columns. We settled into a row of folding chairs just as the strong voices of the male choir to our left rose in song. Drinking in this moment, I allowed pure happiness to wash over me, similar to the sunlight filtering through the stained-glass window behind the altar. The window held the image of a dove, representing the Holy Spirit, the symbol of peace. Peace had truly come to my family and to me. We'd had our share of typical teenage discord in which I could literally hear eye rolls in their voices, car accidents, and pushing boundaries as they grew into young adults (with some tattoos to show for the effort). But we had come through it all as a family, worn in a few places, but stronger for the experiences. I was grateful for that sacred hour that we shared. We were being nourished as a family. Together.

The next day Emily asked to go to the Circus Maximus, the ancient racetrack of the Roman charioteers. Alanna had a full day of classes and would be unable to join us. It was July and Rome was sweltering; I was sweating in places where I didn't even know I had sweat glands. I had twisted my ankle on the cobblestone streets a few days earlier and the combination of the heat and my throbbing ankle caused me to wave Emily on to walk the course herself. I settled under a tree, watching Emily sprint down the steps to the dusty racetrack floor. She stopped every so often to take a photograph. I had gotten my baby to Rome and to the Circus Maximus. She had the dirt of the ancients on her sandals. The sky was robin's egg blue and dotted with billowy white clouds that crowned the flat-topped pine trees. Luckily, tourists congregated at the other steps leading to the track's floor, so I was able to experience this moment of bliss alone. As I stretched my legs in front of me, I realized that I had come a long way, spiritually as well as in miles.

I spent the next-to-last day in Rome alone. Emily had joined Alanna for an overnight stay in the dorm, planning a girls' night out with Alanna's classmates. I was grateful that Emily and I had been able to have some time together before she was set to leave for college, but I also knew that it was important for her to have some time in Italy with people her age. (I was

Serendipity

later shown some beautiful photos of that night, both girls dancing in a fountain where water presses up through the ground. Emily is wearing a blue dress, Alanna a beige one. They are twirling and laughing with friends, apparently just about to be questioned by the Roman polizia. *Did they speak English? And if so, did they see the sign in English that cautioned them to not enter the fountain?)*

I enjoyed my day alone. I sat at an outdoor cafe, people watching and nursing an amazing espresso while savoring a cannoli. Later, I found a small shop for lunch where pizza was weighed and wrapped in paper before being handed over to me. I ate it on a bench alongside some handsome men in suits on their lunch break. I shopped, of course, and then stopped in Saint Peter's to say goodbye to Michelangelo's *Pieta*. After an early dinner and a glass of red wine at a restaurant near the hotel, I walked back to Saint Peter's in the moonlight. Floodlights illuminated the basilica as pilgrims milled about the square. I sat by one of the fountains to clear my mind, wanted to experience the moment. It was as if I were picking up the last of some shells on a beach before departing the seashore. I was gathering the last of my feelings, packing them deep inside me, to bring out like treasure at a later time.

It was still quite warm as I walked back to the hotel, so I stopped to have a glass of prosecco at an outdoor café. Resting my head on the back of the chair, I gazed up at the night sky, at the same moon that had risen over Italy when my ancestors lived there. I took a sip of the sparkling wine and raised my glass to their memory. *Alla famiglia! Grazie!*

I don't think that my great-grandparents had ever made the trip to Rome from their provinces of Benevento and Cosenza and, if they did, it was not for a vacation. They most likely never left their villages until their trip to the port to sail to America. So while I knew that they most likely never toured Rome like the girls and I did, I knew that by bringing my daughters to Italy that we were sharing something with my ancestors.

Although my daughters and I were at the end of our trip, I mused that we were really just at the beginning. Both girls were entering adulthood. I was moving into a new phase of my life, where dreams realized were going to be a standard fare and not a rarity. I often revisit that trip to remind myself of how much my spirit blossomed during those eight days. As I flip through my mental photo album, I pause at the most touching scenes that ironically also happen to be the most mundane: opening up the hotel window to the courtyard below every morning, serenaded by the bells of the church next door; breakfasting on *pan y café*, cheeses, fruits, yogurt, and prosciutto; walking behind the girls as they strolled arm-in-arm, chatting. I would purposely lag behind to watch them, my heart filled with joy. Here were my girls walking through Rome, and I was with them. In another "mind photo," the three of us are having dinner outdoors at a restaurant down a tiny side street close to the Trevi Fountain, off the beaten tourist path. The food was delicious: hand-made pastas, a large green salad with juicy red tomatoes, extra-virgin olive oil, and crusty bread. It wasn't about the food or the beautiful trellis of vines and flowers that provided a canopy through which we viewed the star-filled night sky; it was about being together - in Italy.

This trip was proof to me that I could accomplish anything that I set out to do. I learned that only I was responsible for doing things to make my heart sing. I finally began to understand that when I feed my spirit, when I allow myself to follow my true path in life instead of limiting myself with fear and over-analysis of situations, that my heart expands, my dreams manifest, and I am able to give back to the Universe more fully. I realized that I had been the one stifling my dreams, and that was sobering. I could no longer stand in my life and look around and point at other people or events that had held me back. While some challenging things had certainly happened to me, it was my thoughts surrounding those events that continued to give the events weight long after they had ended. This caused continued suffering and feelings of victimization. I promised myself that I would no longer allow my mind to trump my spirit. If I was meant to do something to nourish my soul, then my mind was going to have to become a servant to my spirit. My mind was going to have to help me find a way to make things happen, not give me a million reasons why I couldn't. This is still an evolving process for me, but this trip to Italy was the start of my pilgrimage in that direction.

Ai sogni di vita-to living dreams!

Souvenirs:

Holy water from Saint Peter's.
Tea towels written in Italian.
A Miraculous Medal and rosary beads.
A scarf that I bought in order to make myself more modest to enter Saint Peter's because my dress was a bit too short. I hadn't heeded Alanna's directive.

CHAPTER 8
JUNIPER STREET

*When the dead are honored and
when the memory of the most distant
ancestor remains alive, the strength of
a people attains its fullest expression.*

Confucius

Filomena rose with the sun. There were many things to do this day and she wanted to tackle the hardest one first. Heading out the door, she walked the narrow streets of Campolattaro. A few of her neighbors were already out and about, headed to the market, sweeping the tiny marble steps in front of their houses, or simply standing in the doorways of their homes talking to passersby. She nodded in the direction of a few women who spoke greetings to her as she passed them, not pausing to engage in conversation, wanting to get to the cemetery as quickly as possible. Entering the church grounds, she moved through the opening in the stone wall to the rows of headstones. Walking the familiar path, it wasn't long before she was at her destination.

Concetta Orsillo Massa. Morta 1905. Riposare in Pace.

Concetta, wife of her son Samuel, died the previous year, leaving behind a husband and five children. Samuel was living in the United States when he received the news of her passing. It had been three years since he last saw his wife and family. He left his village in 1902, landing at Ellis Island before making his way west across Pennsyvania to Falls Creek, where he found work as a stone cutter at the Harvey's Run Quarry. His brother Emilio joined him a few years later in 1904.

Samuel and his wife had an agreement that as soon as the money was raised, Concetta and the children would sail to America. Also agreed was that the family would remain together, which meant that Samuel would not consent to the marriage of any of his three daughters to a man who intended on staying in Campolattaro. If married, the girls would have to remain in Italy with their husbands, and

Serendipity

Samuel could not bear the possibility of never seeing his daughters again. He and Concetta decided that marriage for the girls would have to wait until the family settled in America. There were plenty of men from their village who were working in Falls Creek, from whom they could choose suitors.

He missed his wife and children-Elisa, Leticia, Malvina, Antonio, and Armando-but found comfort in knowing that his mother, Filomena, was helping Concetta raise the children. Concetta and Filomena were not alone in sharing such duties in the absence of a husband. The villages in the province of Benevento in which Campolattaro sat were now devoid of able-bodied men, most of whom had traveled to the States, specifically to the stone quarries of western Pennsylvania or to Philadelphia, where they had *paisano*, or fellow villagers, to help them find jobs and housing.

Filomena gently touched the headstone onto which Concetta's name had been carved.

Samuel says you are his only wife and that he will not marry again. I promise you that I will take care of him and the children. And you take care of my Antonio.

Turning to her left, she focused her attention on another headstone.

Antonio Massa, Morto 1894. Riposare in Pace.

Antonio, her beloved husband. She ran her hand along the top of the stone, remembering how she would sometimes smooth out Antonio's hair before he left the house, brushing a stray piece off his forehead.

My handsome husband. Twelve years since I last saw you. And now it is I who am leaving you. I always thought that one day I would join you here. But God has other plans for me. One day I will see you in heaven, but now Samuel needs me and I must go. I love you.

Filomena surveyed the graveyard. At this early hour she found herself alone, so she wrapped her arms around the headstone in a final hug. She smoothed out the front of her plain black dress and turned to leave. Holding her head high she sighed and walked out of the cemetery.

No more looking back. Life is for the living.

In a few hours Filomena would be traveling to Naples on the first leg of her journey to to be reunited with Samuel and his children in America. She walked with an air of determination through the tiny streets that were flanked on both sides by stone row houses. Her eyes filled with tears that she quickly wiped away with the corner of her sweater. She kicked a stone with the toe of her worn black shoe. What would life in America be like? She walked a few more paces before bending down to pick up the stone she had just kicked, placing it in her pocket. She would take a bit of her village with her to this place called Pennsylvania.

Serendipity

Times were hard financially both in America and in Italy and now, with Concetta gone, she was needed by her son Samuel and his children. The decision to leave her village and to make the transatlantic voyage was not an easy one, but one in which she felt she had no choice. She was unsure how she would make the adjustment to living in a country so far from her homeland, a country in which a different language was spoken, a country with a different political system. She only spoke a regional dialect. And at seventy-two she wondered if she would even survive the voyage, traveling in the deplorable conditions of steerage.

Filomena Casaccio was born in 1834 in the village of Pontelandolfo. Growing up in this mountainous land resplendent with grapes and olives, she developed a natural love of the outdoors. Life was not easy in these villages, and she was raised to value hard work and family. Married and living in the neighboring village of Campolattaro, she had escaped the massacre of over 200 people that befell her village at the hands of Piedmontese occupation troops in 1861.

She had witnessed a lot in her life. She was 36 when Italy became a unified country. Until then, Italy was comprised of a series of states, with Benevento being in the Kindgom of the Two Sicilies. She did not grow up with an allegiance to Italy as the country which we now know but, rather, with an allegiance to the province of Benevento. Her world was small; she had never traveled more than the short distance between her birth village and the village where she made her life as Antonio's wife.

Samuel had returned to Italy in the summer of 1905 to visit his wife's grave and to gather his children to take them to America. Campolattaro held no future for his family and, at age forty-one, he felt as if he was running out of time in which get on solid financial footing. His daughters were of marrying age and he wanted to see them establish their lives near him in Pennsylvania. His two sons, Antonio and Armando, were still young enough to need supervising, which he thought his daughters could handle as they settled into life in America. He hated saying goodbye to his mother, Filomena, that summer, but knew that at her age she had no intention of leaving the village in which she first came to live as a young bride. While her two sons, Samuel and Emilio, were making a new life in America, Filomena's daughter Teresa and her family lived in Campoletarro. She would remain with Teresa.

It was with a heavy heart that Filomena bid farewell to Samuel and the children as they departed for America in the fall of 1905. *Its cruel having to say goodbye to my son twice,* she thought. He had aged since she had last seen him. Lost was the exuberance, replaced now with a weariness. She didn't want to see Samuel struggle to make a living like the few remaining men in the village. If America was his chance at living a happy, prosperous life, then she did not want to stand in his way. Samuel reached out to his mother and gave her a final hug.

"I'm sorry it has to be this way," he said, "but I know you understand that the children and I don't have a life in Italy. I will miss you, I will miss this land, but I have to try to give my children opportunities that they won't have in Benevento."

Filomena walked over to her grandchildren. The girls were trying their best to hide their tears from the grandmother who had raised them to be strong in the face of adversity. *Family first*, she always told them, and now traveling to America with their father and leaving behind their village and their grandmother was putting the needs of the family ahead of their own wants. She gathered the girls around her.

"Be good for your father. Help him, because he has no wife," said Filomena. "Trust who he chooses for your husbands, because he loves you. And I love you, too. The ocean only separates us in distance- the heart knows no separation."

Filomena turned to the little boys, holding the face of each in her hands before bestowing a kiss on their foreheads. Antonio had grown so much in the past few months. At eleven she could see in his face the man he would become, dark-haired and handsome like his grandfather and namesake. Little Armando, only eight, had taken the death of his mother especially hard. He had only a vague memory of living with his father, who had left for America when he was only five. A few nights earlier Armando had whispered to Filomena that he was scared to get on the ship and also frightened to live with Samuel. He asked his grandmother if Samuel knew how to make meatballs, his favorite food. She laughed through her tears. "Well, Armando, your sisters make wonderful meatballs. They learned from the best," she said with a wink. "They will cook for you. Don't worry."

"But I don't want a new mother in America," Armando sobbed, as his head fell onto her chest.

"Armando, be strong for your father. Don't let him see you cry," Filomena said, as she looked into his eyes. "A wife is what your father needs in America. He cannot be alone. A man needs a woman to run the house, to be his companion, to take care of you and Antonio. Trust that God will bring him a good wife in America."

Filomena was aware that Samuel would need to find a new wife in Falls Creek. She knew that when Samuel found this woman she would be younger than him and that she and Samuel would most likely start a family of their own. Filomena had helped

Serendipity

choose Concetta as Samuel's wife. She had to trust in God to send another good woman to Samuel. Little did she know that Samuel would decide that no one could replace Concetta and that he would eventually send a letter requesting that Filomena join him in America to help him raise the children.

Samuel and the children made the trip to the port at Naples without incident. They brought only what could be carried in a few cloth sacks, mainly clothing. The children marveled at the size of their ship, the Napolitan Prince. The crowd began to build as people jostled for position to enter the ship that was bound for Ellis Island. Unbeknownst to them, the Napolitan Prince was notorious for its deplorable conditions. The years between 1880 and 1915 saw over 13 million Italians emigrate from the newly unified country in one of the largest mass exoduses in recorded history, and ships like the Napolitan Prince capitalized on this new market. Samuel's family boarded the ship at the end of the busiest travel period (April through October) for the two-week voyage. He had purchased six third-class tickets at approximately $24 apiece, a lot of money for a man who worked at a stone quarry. The majority of the 1,175 passengers traveled in third-class, or steerage; only two percent, or twenty-five people, traveled in first class.

The children gathered around their father as he was asked a series of questions. Due to the noise, they were only able to hear their father's responses, not the questions themselves. *Samuel Massa, age forty-one, widower, no communicable diseases, yes, my brother Emilio is meeting us in America.* Approved entry onto the ship, they were herded into a berth so tight that there was barely room to turn around. Armando began to cry quietly, catching the attention of Elisa, who protectively wrapped her arm around him. She had become his little mother since the passing of Concetta.

"It's okay. Don't cry. Papa will protect us. What an adventure you are going to have, Armando, sailing on this big ship across the ocean," Elisa comforted.

The ship had five steerage berths, each able to hold 500 people, all located in the hold, the place normally used to carry cargo. They were traveling as a family and so were permitted to lodge together. For two weeks the family ate, slept, and lived in these crampled quarters with little ventilation. They "bathed" having only cold sea water with which to wash. Six toilets were shared with the other 1,150 people in steerage.

Elisa spent the next two weeks wondering and worrying about what would meet her on the other side of the Atlantic. She didn't speak or understand English, she had ever had contact with anyone outside of their village, and most definitely she had never met anyone who had come from another country.

Serendipity

She also knew that within a year she would probably be married.

Having spent the past two weeks in the relative darkness of steerage, surrounded by hundreds of fellow passengers, many of whom were sickened by the conditions of travel, Monday morning, October 16, 1905, loomed bright for the Massa family. They would soon be disembarking at Ellis Island, greeting this new land with the scent of steerage upon them. Ellis Island had only been receiving immigrants for thirteen years when the family landed on its shores. Opened in 1892, the facility was used to weed out those deemed unworthy of entry into America, namely the physically and mentally infirmed and the disabled. Often referred to as the Island of Tears, the passengers feared being denied entrance due an illness, many of which were contracted on the voyage to America. The immigrants were aware that this was the point at which their families could be separated, with some being returned back to their homeland after having endured the long voyage over.

Elisa feared not being able to correctly answer the questions on this side of the Atlantic. The family was tired and scared. Amid the noise and confusion of the 1,000-plus travelers disembarking from the Napolitan Prince, Samuel guided his family into the Registry Hall. Elisa instinctively grabbed the hands of Armando and Antonio while Leticia and Malvina followed. Elisa was trying her best to regain her equilibrium after having spent two weeks at sea. Starting to feel faint she called out for her sister.

"Letizia, I'm afraid I won't make it through inspection. I feel so dizzy," she said.

Rows of immigrants waited on wooden benches for their turn with the inspector. Samuel looked back and saw Elisa losing her balance. He quickly placed her on a bench and directed the rest of the family to sit with her. Nervously tapping his foot, he looked at his watch, hoping that they would be called quickly, before Elisa got sicker. He gazed up at the large American flag which hung at the center of the hall and instinctively began to pray the Hail Mary under his breath.

The Blessed Mother, or Virgin Mary, was very important to Samuel. It was second nature to him to invoke Mary for help and protection. While patron saints played a large role in the lives of most Italians, be they patron saints of villages, occupations, or those for whom the indiviual was named, Samuel had been drawn to Mary from when he was young. He found solace looking up at the small statue of Mary that stood on the dresser in his bedroom. She had a beautiful, youthful face, kind and benevolent. Her tiny hands, open in a receiving gesture, poked out from the long sleeves of her blue gown. She was steadfast, always there. She was the first thing he saw

Serendipity

when he awoke and the last thing he saw before he closed his eyes to sleep.

Please Mother Mary, guide my family through the entry process. You've taken us this far, please, help us, he prayed.

The family must stay together. The large vaulted space of the Registry Hall was noisy and Samuel hoped that the inspectors would be able to hear and also understand what he and his children were saying. He knew that they would only have two minutes each for their entrance interviews. Two minutes that would determine their future. Two minutes to decide whether or not they were healthy enough to enter the country. Two minutes to determine whether they would be deemed a risk to society. Two minutes to determine whether they would remain a family.

The inspectors sat on high chairs, flanked by interpreters. While Ellis Island did their best to provide interpreters for the immigrants, the regional dialects varied and often proved difficult to translate. Immigrants would sometimes find that their surmanes or first names were changed as they were recorded in the registry book. Caught between the noise of the hall and an inability to discern what the new immigrant was saying in an accented response, names were sometimes spelled phoenetically.

The Massa family was called before the inspector, who had the ship's manifest on the table in front of him. Unsmiling, he checked each person against the list, questioning Samuel intensely. Any bit of hesitancy on anwering the questions would result in the family being detained. Samuel took a deep breath and quickly rolled off the answers. Satisfied with the responses to the questions, the inspector directed the family to the station for their medical inspections.

Known as the "six-second phyicals," these hurried exams were meant to weed out those who had infectious diseases or other infirmities that would make them a burden to society. Those who failed the physical faced immediate deportation or a quarantine that could last up to six weeks. Armando looked back at his father, his lip quivering, as he was summoned before the medical inspector. Samuel nodded his head in the direction of the uniformed inspector, gesturing that Armando should proceed. Armando pulled away as the inspector used a buttonhook to lift his eyelid, looking for evidence of trachoma, a communicable eye disease. Elisa, still feeling unsteady on her feet, braced herself against the metal pole that supported the rope railing that separated the immigrants. Samuel held his breath as each child was examined. He went last for the exam and heaved a sigh of relief as he was handed landing cards for the family. All told, the process had taken five hours. The children were tired and hungry-and

Serendipity

relieved. They were permitted to leave Ellis Island and begin their new life in the United States. Samuel kissed each of his five children. He thought he saw his wife, Concetta, out of the corner of his eye.

I'm so exhausted that now I am seeing ghosts, he thought.

It was only then that he realized he had really just caught a side glimpse of Elisa. She had grown into a woman during the time he had been in America. Although she would always remain his *figlia*, or daughter, he could not deny that she was now a young woman. She had what he called "laughing eyes," sparkling and happy.

She looks just like her mother did when I took her as my bride, he observed.

He knew that within a short period of time he would lose his beloved daugther to another man, a man who was working in the quarry this very moment in Falls Creek, a particular man he had in mind. As the children gathered their possessions, Samuel was mindful that the Blessed Mother had answered his prayers. They were all together, ready to begin life anew in America.

Thank you, Mother Mary, he mouthed as they entered into the sunlight.

The family took the ferry from Ellis Island directly into the hustle and bustle of New York City. The children had never been in a city of this size before. It made Naples seem small in comparison. Instinctively, they clung together with their belongings in the middle of the circle they had formed. Samuel left them on the sidewalk with the admonition to stay put and darted into a small shop selling bread and cheese. He walked up to the wooden counter and asked for a piece of the round cheese and a loaf of crusty bread. The family ate their first meal in America as they slowly made their way to the station to catch the train that would take them to western Pennsylvania and Falls Creek. Exhausted, they fell into the seats, each using their traveling companion as a pillow.

Incorporated only five years earlier, Falls Creek had been a meeting place for some of the worst criminals in Pennsylvania after the Civil War. However, with the coming of the railroad, it was transitioning into a respectable place in which to raise a family. The town was a major source of sandstone that was used in construction of railroads and railroad bridges. One of the largest quarries was run by former stone cutter Giuseppe Gocella, who used his connections to his homeland to recruit men from the region of Benevento to work in the quarry. Benevento was renowned for its stone cutters, and these men were a valuable commodity to Gocella. Samuel and his brother Emilio had followed their *paisanos* to Falls Creek to work in the quarries.

Serendipity

Emilio anxiously paced the station's platform as he waited for the train that carried his brother and his family. As the train pulled into the station with a thunderous roar, everyone knew their lives would never be the same. Samuel gathered his children and their belongings. Emilio stepped up to the door to help them off the train.

"I'm glad you made it safely," Emilio spoke softly as he reached for the hands of his brother's family.

The boys bounded off the train, happy to be able to stretch their legs, with the girls following close behind. Emilio and Samuel hugged and led the way, walking deep in conversation. Emilio separated from the group when they reached Samuel's house. The homes in Falls Creek were nothing like the houses in Campoletarro; they were made of wood, not stone. The family entered the house and dropped their belongings on the floor of the front room as they glanced around at their new home. Today they would rest. Tomorrow they began their life in America.

One night a few weeks later, Samuel approached Elisa as she sat in a worn armchair mending Antonio's pants which he had ripped on a tree branch earlier that day. The house was quiet-as everyone else had gone to bed.

"I know you won't be under my roof much longer," Samuel said as he faced his daughter. "The eligible men at the quarry will soon be interested in courting such a fine young woman. I promise you that I will select only the most honest, hard-working, respectful man for you to take as a husband. Trust me."

She nodded. "I do, Papa. I know you only want the best for me."

"Wait here," he said. He returned from his bedroom with a small porcelain statue of the Blessed Mother. It had been years since she had seen the statue of the youthful Virgin. She remembered that it had always been on the dresser in the bedroom of her parents.

"On my last trip to home, your mother wrapped this statue in tissue and insisted that I bring it back with me to America. She prayed to the Blessed Mother every night to look after me until she could join me in America and take care of me as her husband. It was the last time I saw your mother."

Samuel grew silent as his finger traced the face of the statue.

"This will become yours one day. I want the Blessed Mother to look after you as you begin your own family. Always remember to keep her in your life. Pray to her. She hears your prayers. She understands what it is to be a mother and a wife. Keep her close to you."

"Thank you, Papa, I will. I love you so much."

"Thank you, Elisa, for helping me with the children. Now, put down that mending and get some sleep. Your brothers have had a headstart on you and they will be awake sooner than you think," he said, winking.

Elisa missed not having a mother who she would be able to go to for advice when she became a married woman, a prospect that was not far off. Samuel had chosen Giuseppe Greco, a foreman at the Falls Creek Quarry, as her husband. He introduced the two shortly after Elisa's arrival. Giuseppe was an attractive man, with dark hair, brown eyes, and a mustache. He too had left Benevento a few years earlier due to lack of work in the villages. His hard work caught the attention of Mr. Gocella, the quarry's owner and enabled him to quickly rise through the ranks. Elisa grew to like Giuseppe in the little time they spent together.

Christmas was approaching and Samuel decided to invite Giuseppe to the family's Christmas Eve dinner, *la Vigilia di Natale*, the vigil of the birth of Jesus. As the calendar turned to December Elisa found herself growing more homesick. Of course it would be nice to celebrate Christmas with her father; he had missed the last few Christmases with the family. But she greatly missed her mother. One evening after dinner she quietly left the house for a few minutes to stand in the front yard. She could hear the boys inside talking excitedly about the approaching holiday. She was glad to hear them conversing in English. She wanted them to assimilate into their new country.

She took a few steps away from the house. The night was cold and clear. She drew her shawl closer to her thin body. It was her first Christmas without her mother and she missed her especially as the holiday approached. It was her mother's favorite holiday. Concetta loved cooking the traditional southern Italian Christmas Eve meal of the seven fishes. Preparing this large meal would fall on Elisa to orchestrate this year. She had always helped her mother and grandmother with this event, doing their bidding as they'd wave a floured hand toward something they wanted her to fry or stir. She knew she couldn't bring back her mother, but she wished that her grandmother, her *nona*, Filomena, was living with the family in America.

Looking up at the midnight blue sky, she picked the brightest star and made a wish. *I miss Nona so much. I wish that she can feel my love right now and ask this star to bring it to her.* She had loved the stars for as long as she could remember. When her father was far away in America she would talk to him through the stars.

From starry skies descending-she remembered the opening words to one of her favorite songs, "Tu Scendi dalle Stelle," a song sung at midnight on Christmas Eve to welcome the coming of the Christ Child. She ached for her old life in Italy with her mother and grandmother; sometimes the ache turned into a physical pain in her stomach as she longed to feel safe in the arms of these women. She loved being with her father, but the reason for the reunion also caused such sadness.

She looked around the front yard of Samuel's house which had been neglected over the years. Having arrived too late in the season to tend to the garden, Elisa was determined to bring the garden back to life in the spring. She was raised around beautiful plants and flowers and wanted to recreate that for the family in America.

I'll have the boys help me clean this yard and plant beautiful flowers for the family to enjoy. We'll set down our roots in America.

One evening as Christmas Eve approached, Elisa gathered her younger sisters, Leticia and Malvina, around the well-worn wooden dining table. Recipes were learned by watching the cook. Nothing was measured and no recipe was written down, as most women of the generations of her mother and grandmother were illiterate.

"I want us to make Mommy proud with our Christmas Eve dinner. The boys and Daddy deserve to be fed the way Mommy would see to it. I'm hoping that the three of us will be able to remember how Mommy and Nona cooked the seven fishes," said Elisa.

"We live in the mountains of Pennsylvania, Elisa. Where are we going to buy seafood?," asked Leticia.

"Papa says the men make sure the fish get to Falls Creek," she laughed.

Pulling out a piece of used brown paper, Elisa made a list, baccala (cod fish), smelts, anchovies, sardines, mussels, and clams.

"That's only six," observed Malvina. "We need seven. What are we missing?"

The girls studied the list in silence.

"Calamari!" they exclaimed in unison.

It was the first time Elisa had seen her sisters excited since landing in America a few months earlier. They would work together as a team, with Elisa as the lead, to bring *La Vigilia* to Falls Creek.

In the days before Christmas, Elisa instructed her siblings in the cleaning of the house and the decorating of it with sprigs of evergreen that they cut from the surrounding trees. The creche took center stage on the sideboard. It was one of the most precious items that the family brought with them from Italy. Painted clay figures of the Virgin Mary and Saint Joseph flanked an empty manger. Figures of a shepherd, a cow, a donkey, and three sheep rounded out the scene in the wooden creche. An ceramic angel dressed in pink, wings open in majesty, was placed at the top of the creche. Tiny pieces of straw were scattered on the floor of the creche. Elisa had hidden

Serendipity

the baby Jesus behind the creche to be brought out with great ceremony at midnight on Christmas Day. The three wise men, or Magi, were also tucked behind the creche, to be brought out on January 6, the Epiphany.

A bowl of almonds and cashews was placed on the dining table, along with a metal nutcracker and pick. Dried figs stuffed with walnuts were placed on the sideboard. The girls had prepared *zeppole*, fried dough balls, and assorted cookies for dessert. The Anisette liquer was taken down from the shelf and placed next to the cookies. Things were starting to fall into place.

Elisa knew that her work on Christmas Eve would begin early with the cleaning of the fish. She felt pressure to perfectly time the cooking so that all of the food came to the table hot, at the same time. She was so preoccupied with the preperations that she had almost forgotten to be nervous about hosting Giuseppe for the *Vigilia*. Almost. She wanted to make her father proud and impress her future husband.

She rose before daylight on Christmas Eve. Coming down the wooden stairs she heard her father and Uncle Emilio enter the house. They had wrapped packages of fish. "You doubted Papa, didn't you?" Samuel joked as he winked at Elisa. "The fish have swum all the way to Falls Creek just for your meal." The men laughed as they dropped the packages near the wood stove. Giving each other a parting hug, Emilio wished Elisa good luck with the preparation of the meal.

As her sisters joined her in the kitchen, Elisa found herself naturally falling into the role of chief cook. She heard her mother's voice in her directions to her sisters to stir and fry. Samuel took the boys out for most of the day to have them run off their excitement.

It took the girls most of the afternoon to cook the meal. As the finishing touches were put on the dishes, each sister took a turn going upstairs to freshen up and to change from clothes that reeked of fried fish into a clean dress, with Elisa going last. Pausing to straighten the flatware, she surveyed the scene one last time before hurrying upstairs. No sooner had she finished brushing her hair and pushing the final hairpin into place than she heard her father's voice warmly welcoming Giuseppe into his home. "Samuel, please call me Joseph. I'm in America now," Giuseppe laughed as he hugged Samuel.

Elisa modestly avoided the stares of her assembled family as she descended the stairs. Everyone knew why Joseph was invited to the *Vigilia*, the most important meal of the year. Samuel sat at the head of the table and asked everyone to take a seat.

"Please bow your heads as we thank our Father for this food. I am honored to host this meal on

Serendipity

Christmas Eve. It is the first time in many years that I am able to share it with my children. We all remember our loved ones who are no longer able to sit with us at this table, including my beautiful wife, Concetta, may they rest in peace. I would like to extend a warm welcome to Giuseppe, oh I'm sorry, Joseph, and to thank my daughters for preparing such a delicious dinner. Let us raise our glasses. *A famiglia!*"

Chatter and laughter soon filled the room as the serving dishes were passed around. Samuel looked around the table and felt blessed that he and his children had made the trip safely to America and that everyone seemed to be assimilating into their new country. The house was once again filled with joy and laughter, and for that he was grateful. He knew the children missed their mother; he missed his own mother in a similar way. He could see her sitting on the wooden chair in their small garden in Italy. He knew he would never be able to spend another Christmas with her and sent her a silent wish for a *Buon Natale.*

"Papa, it's almost midnight." The sound of Armando's voice jolted Samuel back to Falls Creek.

"Well, then, we'd better assemble at the creche, shouldn't we?" Samuel said as he rose from the table.

Everyone followed him, gathering around the table in the front parlor on which the tiny wooden creche sat. Tradition had it that at midnight the youngest in the family would place the figure of the baby Jesus in the manger while serenaded by the family. Samuel placed the clay figure in Armando's outstretched hands, the hands of a child. He looked into his son's eyes. *He is still so young*, Samuel thought, *a baby himself.*

Standing on tiptoes, Armando gently placed the baby in the manger in the creche. The family began to sing:

Tu scendi dalle stele
O Re del Cielo
E vieni in una grotto
Al freddo al gelo

From starry skies descending...

Elisa was embarrassed at the escaped tear that traveled down her cheek. So much had changed in the past six months: she lost her mother, she had to leave her grandmother behind in Italy, and she traveled across the Atlantic to start a new life in America, and now, to the right of her father stood Giuseppe, a man she would be marrying in a few months. She caught the attention of her father, who noticed her quickly wipe away the tears and resume her singing.

Serendipity

Her mother and grandmother would be so proud of the woman she has become.

Joseph courted Elisa over the next few months. He would come to dinner every Sunday so that Elisa could impress him with her cooking skills. Joseph was especially fond of Elisa's "gravy" or red sauce, that covered her homemade ravioli and gnocchi. After dinner they retired to the front room, where they were chaperoned by the entire family. A short time later, in early 1906, they were married in Falls Creek. Joseph was thirty, Elisa was twenty. Each dressed in their Sunday best and met at the Catholic church for the nuptial Mass. A small luncheon, cooked by Elisa's sisters, followed the ceremony.

Joseph continued as foreman at the quarry, working even harder, as he was now a married man with a wife to support. They set up house a few blocks from where Samuel and the children lived. Elisa's small, wood-framed home was her pride and joy. She found herself constantly cleaning, frustrated by the dust from the unpaved streets that seemed to constantly fill the home. The wooden sidewalks did little to help matters and when it rained she was no match for the mud. But she was happy as Joseph's wife and eagerly looked forward to starting her family. On New Year's Eve, 1906, assisted by a midwife, Elisa gave birth at home to her first child, a beautiful little girl they named Maria, or Mary, after Joseph's mother.

Shortly after the birth, Samuel and the children arrived to greet the newest family member. Samuel entered the bedroom first. Elisa was sitting up in the bed holding the baby. Joseph excused himself to give Samuel some time alone with his daughter. Samuel pulled a wooden chair up to the bed and leaned over to kiss Elisa on the cheek. His lips touched a tear.

"Oh, Papa, how can I be so happy and so sad at the same time?" Elisa asked barely above a whisper. She didn't want Joseph to hear her. "I love this little baby and my husband but I miss Mama so much. And I miss Nona. I wish she could be here with me. They will never get to meet my children."

"I know, *figlia*," he said. "I miss them too. When she is a little bigger and stronger, and the weather is warmer, bring Maria outside and introduce her to Mama and Nona under the stars."

"And introduce her to your other mother, too," Samuel said.

Elisa looked at him quizzically. "Who do you mean?"

"Here, this is for you. Keep her on your dresser," he responded as he pulled the statue of the Blessed Mother out from under his coat.

"You should have her now to protect your family. Your mother would want that. Pray to her, ask her for help, thank her for the wonders she will bring you. Cry to her in silence when you are scared or

Serendipity

overwhelmed. She will guide you. And you've named that beautiful baby after her as well."

Samuel rose and placed the statue in the center of the dresser. "Now, let me call in your sisters. They are anxious to meet the niece they have promised to spoil. Then we'll let in the boys. We don't want to overwhelm little Maria," he laughed.

Over the next few months Samuel grappled with a problem. With his daughters Leticia and Malvina soon betrothed, he realized that he would need help raising his sons. He had no intention of remarrying and he knew that the boys needed a female presence in the home. With a bit of trepidation he sat down and wrote a letter to his mother, Filomena, requesting that she come to America to help him raise his sons. It was a letter written in desperation. He didn't want the boys falling in with a bad crowd. He needed his mother's help more than ever. He was well aware of her age. At seventy-two, she might not survive the voyage to America. He was asking a lot of her, asking her to leave behind her village and her only daughter, Teresa.

When the letter arrived in Italy, Filomena, who was illiterate, had to take it to the priest to read it to her. She sat in stunned silence, but was relieved that the letter was not a harbinger of bad news. Realizing that she had a life-altering decision to make, she remained in the church to pray for guidance. When she returned home she told Teresa about Samuel's request. Teresa and her husband, Antonio Caiazzo, decided that they would travel to America with Filomena and start a new life. The family would not be broken apart.

Filomena was able to be with Elisa for the birth of her second daughter, Nilda, in 1908. More children followed with Biasino (1910), Samuel (1911), Joseph (1914) and, lastly, Philomena (1916), named after Elisa's beloved grandmother, Filomena. A few years after her arrival in Falls Creek, Filomena and Samuel left with Armando and Antonio for Philadelphia, where some extended family had settled. The quarries were losing business and Samuel decided to connect with family who had businesses working on funeral monuments in the City of Brotherly Love.

Things were looking up for Joseph and Elisa, though. When Mr. Gocella decided to move to another town-and a larger home, he invited the Greco family to live in his former house. It was one of the finest in the small town and Elisa was glad to settle there in 1916 while awaiting the birth of her sixth child. Six months after Philomena was born, Joseph developed pneumonia. He recuperated at home with Elisa taking care of him and the six children. Against his doctor's orders Joseph left the home one evening to pay a call to the town's shoemaker, whose son had been killed earlier that day by a railroad car.

Serendipity

His illness quickly progressed to double pneumonia and he died within days. Twelve years after arriving in America, Elisa found herself widowed at the age of thirty-one with six children under her care.

She made the decision to move her family to Philadelphia to be close to her father and grandmother. One month after Joseph's death, Elisa and the children boarded the train to Philadelphia, relieved that her sister Malvina's husband, Antonio Paolella, a stone cutter who had worked with Joseph in Falls Creek, invited the family to live with them while they sorted out matters. Malvina, Antonio, Elisa, and their combined brood of thirteen children would live in a tiny, six-room rowhouse consisting of three bedrooms, one bathroom, a kitchen, and a downstairs living space on Juniper Street in South Philadelphia. Samuel and Filomena lived on the same street and were able to help Elisa with the children.

Elisa worked from home doing piecework, bits of sewing, to support her family. The children were educated through eighth grade at Saint Rita's parish school. They were then expected to work to help support the family. Joseph especially took to working with stone like his father and grandfather, excelling at stone carving.

With hard work and frugal living, Elisa was able to save enough money to purchase a house on

Juniper Street. As she stood on the doorstep of her new home, memories flooded back: her mother's face, the embrace of Filomena when they were reunited in Falls Creek, holding Joseph's hand as he passed. One of the first things she could afford to purchase for her new home was a concrete statue of the Blessed Mother for the garden in the small backyard.

Elisa was so proud of what she had accomplished and also of the fine young men her sons had become without a father's influence. She was a loving but strict mother who knew she had to help her sons avoid the temptation of making quick money by running numbers or doing other errands for *La Costa Nostra*. Her daughters were her other source of pride, and together, through all of the hardships, they had remained a family. She crossed the threshold of her house on Juniper Street, the first woman in her family to own a house.

A few years ago I was helping my mother prepare for my father's funeral. His sudden passing had left the family reeling. He was the heart of our family, the voice ringing out in laughter, the man of reason, the hand of encouragement, and the patriarch. So much of who I am was molded by my father. And now

Serendipity

he was gone, seemingly vanishing into thin air. His possessions were still where he left them. His nightstand held his glasses, his radio, his hearing aid, and the silver circular rosary that he used to pray every evening.

I was assembling a photo montage of his life when I came across a black-and-white photograph of a woman, hair pulled into a bun, sitting outdoors on a wooden bench. Roses climbed on a trellis behind her. She was dressed in all in black. The woman in the photograph was Elisa, my father's grandmother and my great-grandmother. I heard that she wore black for the rest of her life following the death of her husband, Joseph. Elisa called my father Josie, not Joseph. He was her oldest grandchild, named after her late husband, and he was her favorite.

I think about my father every day, continuing to talk to him and ask him for guidance. I also think about my grandparents and great-grandparents, who are also gone, but only in the physical sense. Who were these people whose traditions I still maintain? What else did I inherit from them besides my name? How was the spirit of my ancestors a part of me? How was their energy still present in my life? What traits of theirs did I possess?

I had only a very limited knowledge of the lives of Filomena and Elisa but soon after my father's passing I began to research the family, wanting to know the people whose images I came across in the photographs. I joined Ancestry.com and did some genealogical research on the family. It was challenging, especially because the spelling of first and last names seemed to change on every census. Elisa, for instance, was sometimes referred to as Alice on census records. I guess it depended on how well the person taking the census information understood a woman speaking in broken English. Undeterred, I continued my research. I was able to assemble a pretty thorough picture of the villages in Italy from which they emigrated, what ships brought them to the United States, where they lived, when they settled, when they were born and died, who they married, the names of their children, and what they did for a living. But the statistics told me nothing about the people-about how they lived, what their personalities were like, their hopes and dreams and fears, their triumphs and heartbreaks. For that I had to remember the stories told by my grandparents around the Sunday dinner table, stories that I had forgotten over time as I raised my own children.

I received my Confirmation in 1968 when I was nine years old. I had to pick a Confirmation name, the name of a saint who would serve as a heavenly protector. My mother wanted me to pick the name Elizabeth. I, however, wanted to choose the name Elisa. I had always like that name, it was the name of my aunt who was to be my Confirmation sponsor. My mother relented and I was confirmed Anne Elisa. It wasn't until later that I learned it was also the name of my paternal great-grandmother, after whom my aunt was named.

During what might be termed a midlife inventory, I decided to drive to Elisa's house on Juniper Street to visit her prized possession. I was seeking some strength from Elisa and Filomena, and Elisa's house was a touchstone, a symbol of resilience. It's a tiny brick row house in South Philadelphia in what is now considered a much sought-after location. Filomena's house was across the street. I drove down the tiny street and parked in front of Elisa's house. Trees shaded the street which was devoid of people due to the heat of the July day. I exited the car and stood in the middle of the street, moving my glance between both houses. I imagined Elisa and Filomena meeting outside on the steps to talk. I could see Elisa's children running between the houses.

Elisa and Filomena were strong women, not afraid of picking up and moving on after life had thrown them some pretty big challenges. Like Elisa, I too raised my children without a father in the home. Sometimes I'd be bone tired, but life went on. I parented alone during disagreements with teenagers. I had two children. Elisa had six. We both managed with the help of extended family. We both raised children of whom we could be proud, children who learned the importance of valuing and respecting family.

Did I inherit Filomena's bravery? She began a new life at age seventy-two. Would I be able to conjure up the bravery to actually do things that I knew would make me happy but involved changing my present life in some pretty drastic ways? As I make those turtle steps of change, I call upon the spirits of Filomena and Elisa to assist me.

I walked up to what was Elisa's house. The three marble steps leading to the front door were sparkling white but worn in the center from over a century of use. These were the steps that my grandfather and great-grandmother navigated on a daily basis; the ones they sat on in the evening to enjoy a breeze or converse with family and neighbors. I ran my hand over the cool marble and then tentatively sat on them.

A woman opened the front door of the house. I jumped up, afraid that she would trip over me as she began to step outside. I apologized for startling her and explained why I was sitting on her front steps. She paused in the doorway. Believing I wasn't a threat, she invited me to have a look inside the house.

My great-aunts Nilda and Philomena, both spinsters, continued to live in the house with Elisa after

Serendipity

the other children had married and left. They continued to live in the house after Elisa's death. I visited the house often as my parents took us to spend time with my great-aunts. I remember what the interior of the house looked like, the front parlor that had large glass doors to shut it off from the rest of the house. This was the room into which my cousins and I would be deposited as the grown-ups took coffee in the dining room. We children would sit in this tiny room and play, never thinking to bother the grown-ups. Eventually, we would be invited to the table for some cookies before being sent back to the front room to continue entertaining ourselves. After a while we would grow tired and all find a space on the two couches to lie down. I remember falling asleep to the sound of the clinking of coffee cups on saucers and of laughter and adult conversations sprinkled with Italian phrases. I can still recall my father picking me up at the end of the evening, my face sticking to the plastic that covered the couch, to carry me to the car for the ride home.

I remember the dining room of that house and the large table around which the family gathered. I can remember being there for Christmas visits and being shown the crèche on the sideboard, the very one that was brought to Falls Creek all those years ago. I remember the tiny kitchen in the back of the house and the even smaller backyard. But I don't remember being told anything about Elisa or Filomena as a child.

I politely declined the kind woman's invitation to tour her house, preferring to remember it in my own way. I was certain the house had been renovated in HGTV fashion to have an open floor plan, granite kitchen countertops, and stainless steel appliances. If I saw the house in its present state it would no longer be Elisa's house in my mind. I got in the car and drove home.

My mother has been asking for over a year that I return the family photographs I borrowed for my father's funeral. I sift through them one last time. At the bottom of the pile I find a black-and-white photograph of me as a child, three years old, standing with my mother, sister, and Aunt Nilda in what I now recognize as the backyard of Elisa's home. We are assembled in what seems to be the same spot that Elisa's photograph was taken many years earlier. I set aside the photograph to keep.

Martin's car pulls into the driveway and I go outside to greet him. We walk into the back garden to check on the newly planted rose bushes. My yard is over an acre, so much larger than Elisa's, but we share the same love of gardening. Nestled under the hydrangea is the concrete statue of the Blessed Mother that I inherited from my grandparents, the one that Elisa bought for her yard. It's May and, as

Serendipity

is tradition, I've placed a garland of flowers around the Virgin's head for her crowning.

I've carried on a lot of these traditions, like the Christmas Eve feast of the seven fishes, placing the Baby Jesus in the manger at midnight on Christmas Eve, and a devotion to the Virgin Mary. But I've inherited so much more than tradition-I've inherited a strong sense of family and the value of hard work. More importantly I realize that I've been inherited a strong faith and resiliency that I know will serve me well, if the past is any indicator.

<u>Souvenirs:</u>

I asked the woman who now lives in Elisa's house if there were roses growing in her garden. She said the old rose bushes were the pride of her garden. I asked her for a few roses which she happily gave me. I placed one rose in front of Elisa's statue of the Blessed Mother that is in my garden. I pressed the other two roses in a book.

CHAPTER 9
FEAR AND YOGA IN NEW JERSEY

The practice of yoga itself transforms.

Ravi Ravindra

I did it for first time on a linoleum floor under fluorescent lights. I hated it and vowed never to do it again.

Yoga.

When I was a teenager, aerobics were *the* way to exercise. I'd put on my leg warmers and leotards to "feel the burn," as Jane Fonda directed. Years later, a new generation, including my daughter Emily, wanted to try yoga. But she didn't want to attend yoga classes held at the local high school alone. I signed up to keep her company, but to me it conjured up images of uncomfortable pretzel-like contortions. I bought a yoga mat and finally had a legitimate reason to wear yoga pants. Our class was advertised as Beginner Yoga, but when we arrived for the first session we found out that our class had been merged with the advanced class due to low enrollment. Denied a basic introduction to yoga, Emily and I were thrown into the various poses. We tried our best to keep up with the advanced students. Well, *I* was trying to keep up. Emily adapted quickly and easily. But of course, she was seventeen years old and still limber.

I silently cursed the instructor as she held us in cobra pose way too long. Had she forgotten that I was a novice or was she a sadist? If I had been with a group of beginners, the class might have gone a different way for me, although I'm sure I still would have complained about cobra pose. I tried really hard to keep up, but after the fifth sun salutation, I wanted to collapse. The instructor finally moved the class back to a floor position. I wiped the sweat from my eyes and looked over at Emily next to me. She shot me a Zen-like smile as she expertly maintained her pigeon pose.

It was a horrible introduction to yoga, yet for some reason I came away wanting to practice more- but in a different setting. Practicing in a gym-like setting seemed to treat yoga primarily as a form of exercise versus a moving meditation. I began to read books and articles to deepen my understanding of what yoga actually is. I watched videos and was inspired by seeing practices in tranquil settings, the poses enhanced by soft music. Emily was content to continue her practice at home, using videos for guidance. I, however, signed up for classes at a local yoga studio and learned the difference between Yin, Vinyasa, and Restorative yoga. I was introduced to meditation, chanting, and breathing exercises.

My yoga instructors referred to the classes as *practices* and I was asked to set a *sankalpa* or "intention" at the beginning of each session. The intention could be one word to which to dedicated my practice, a word that symbolized a value I wanted to bring into my life, such as love, compassion, forgiveness, tolerance, acceptance, release, or patience. I usually chose a different intention for each class, depending on what I felt I needed to focus on in my life at that moment. We practiced "opening" poses, whether for the heart, the hips, or even the throat. The poses were meant to enhance flexibility and also to counter the negative effects of sitting too long at work or maintaining an incorrect posture.

Serendipity

But they were more than stretching exercises; they also opened the body's energy channels to promote improved physical and mental health. Throughout these "openings," I would allow the intention behind the *sankalpa* to seep into me. I gave myself the gift of 90 minutes to experience the feelings behind the word.

I was exposed to the practice of being present, of living in the moment, of being mindful, of being aware of my thoughts: all new concepts to me. I realized that yoga was more than a form of exercise. What I had been referring to as yoga, namely the postures and poses, called *asana*, was only one component. Other parts included *yamas* (ethical guidelines regarding moral behavior toward others), *niyamas* (ethical guidelines regarding moral behavior toward yourself), *pranayama* (breathing exercises), *pratyahara* (the withdraw from negativity), *dharana* (concentration and focus), *dhyana* (meditation), and *samadhi* (enlightenment or merging of the self with the Universe). As I learned that yoga also involves mind and spirit, my practice expanded to include more than physical poses.

Yoga was transformative. I started feeling healthier, calmer, and more aware of the emotions I was bringing with me into various life situations. I became less defensive, for example, when I was attacked by someone through harsh words or actions, choosing to see instead that this attack reflected more about the other person than about me. I didn't react to negative situations as quickly, choosing instead to create spaces, pauses between my thoughts and my actions, a cushion, so to speak, that saved me from injuring myself or others with my reactions to events or words. I worked on meeting resistance in another person with a form of yielding rather than exerting just as much force back, which usually resulted in loggerheads, anger, or stress. That bit of yielding, even if I just took a few seconds to send that person thoughts of love and kindness, seemed to psychically catch the person off guard and diffuse the situation. Of course, I am still human, so these practices continue to take time to embed in my life-and I don't always succeed in meeting negativity with love. But I continue to *practice*.

Yoga also encouraged me to push beyond self-imposed boundaries in a gentle way, not in the over-the-top way of the boot camp-style that I experienced in my introduction to yoga. Yoga is noncompetitive; I wasn't trying to beat someone's time or keep up with the class. In fact, the teacher always reminded us that if a pose proved to be too difficult or hurt, we should feel free to release it. There would be time again in another practice to settle into the pose a little deeper, when our bodies might be a little more yielding. There was no judgment. It was all good-or

Serendipity

so I thought. Until I found out that yoga could be harmful to me.

Driving home from work one evening in January, I was bombarded with radio warnings of an imminent snowstorm that was traveling up the East Coast. For the unfamiliar, when weather forecasters predict a snowstorm in New Jersey, it generally doesn't amount to more than a few snowflakes. What can be measured are the increased viewing ratings of the local newscasts. The prospect of snow sends radio and television stations into their Winter Storm Updates. Viewers watch newscasters deliver their ominous predictions while dump trucks behind them beep and buzz, filling their loads with road salt. Then the scene shifts to a grocery store where anxious shoppers pile their carts with necessities like bread and milk. The final scene before commercial break is at the hardware store, where the camera scans the empty shelves to show that there are no more snow shovels, snow blowers, or salt for walkways. Snow and sleet and ice-oh my!

Entering the house, I called my mother, one of the storm worriers, who was recovering from pneumonia.

"Hi, Mom. Do you need anything from the grocery store or the pharmacy? Do you need any prescriptions filled? Any last-minute groceries?"

No, apparently she didn't need anything. She had sent my father out earlier in the day to gather the provisions that they rarely eat-bread and milk. I then asked about my father, who has a bad back and limited mobility. I had nightmares of him navigating the backyard to bring in firewood while balancing on his cane.

"Does Daddy have enough wood in the house for the fireplace?"

"Yes, Daddy has enough wood," she replied. "Thanks for asking, honey. Are you home from work?"

"Yeah, Mom, I'm home."

"Are the curtains closed? Did you take your keys out of the door? Is the alarm on?"

She was going over her fear checklist, which reminded me of a pilot before take-off. Since my husband was away and the girls were at college, she knew I was alone. My mother would like me to literally barricade myself in my home every night. To be fair, I did make the mistake of telling her that a few times I had entered the house with my arms full and inadvertently left my keys in the front door-for the entire night. To her, it was a neon sign, an open invitation to any passing thief.

"Mom, it's only six o'clock. I have to run out as soon as I change. Believe it or not, I need bread for lunch tomorrow."

"Do you want your father to get you the bread?"

And there's the beauty of my family. We had gone full circle.

Serendipity

I love my mother. She is supportive, caring, and loving. It's just that she tends to focus *a bit* on worst-case scenarios. I joke with her about it all the time. She injects me with these mini-doses of anxiety: *Are the girls safe at college? Do you have enough money to survive?*

"No, Mom, I don't want Daddy to go to the store for me. Please, stop with all these fears. Why is everything always so negative? It drives me crazy."

By now, I was beginning to regret calling because I was tired and cranky and the conversation seemed to have taken a downward turn. I had called to ask her if she needed help, not to upset her.

"I'm sorry," she replied sarcastically. "I only want you to be safe. I worry about you."

I wanted to ask her if she knew that the word "worry" came from an Old English word meaning to bind, squeeze, or strangle. (She probably did, because she liked to read the dictionary.) I wanted to ask her if worry had ever stopped something negative from happening. I wanted to ask her if worry had caused unnecessary stress. I wanted to ask her if worry had, in fact, diminished to some extent the really good things that happen. I wanted to ask. But I was tired and I really just wanted to end the call.

"Okay, Mom. Thanks for the concern. I'm sorry I snapped. I'll call you tomorrow. I love you."

I hung up the phone and climbed the stairs to my bedroom and turned on the television while changing clothes. Pulling on a sweatshirt, I heard a report of a woman killed on a road that I had traveled earlier in the day. She had been stopped at a traffic light when a car making a left turn cut off a dump truck that happened to be next to her. The load of salt for the impending storm shifted, causing the truck to tip, crushing the woman and her SUV. I realized it could have been me. It could have been anyone. Should I now be afraid to drive? Sighing, I walked back downstairs, deciding to forgo the bread and a trip to the grocery store with the frenzied shoppers.

I peeked through the closed curtains. No snow. Settling into the sofa, I opened the *New York Times*. An article immediately caught my attention, warning how yoga could damage the body. It listed horrible injuries suffered by some yoga practitioners who pushed their bodies too far. I found myself growing angry because the article was poking holes in something that was important to me, a practice that contributed to my tranquility and good health. It touched a nerve because it was further evidence of the many ways I found myself bombarded daily, whether by the media or from the people who felt that I should live in fear of everything. Terrorists, solar flares, diet soda, mosquito bites, snow, and now, apparently, yoga.

I began my yoga practice to exercise my body, but I continued practicing to still my mind. The

Serendipity

challenge for me is to practice not worrying about the future or beating myself up over past events. I'm learning to face my fears by shining the light of mindfulness on the dark corners of my mind. I try to patch up the unseen cracks and crevices in my soul through which the invasive, fearful beliefs threaten to invade. Usually, what I fear is not occurring in my present-I've projected it to my future or conjured up something from my past. So, it can't be true, because the future is not real and the past doesn't exist. I understand that the real threats are fear and anxiety. It is these that I need to guard against, that I need to lock out of my psyche and my body. These are the true thieves that threaten to steal my precious life.

Finished with the article on yoga, I meant to toss the newspaper onto the coffee table but missed. The newspaper fell into a basket to the side of the table that held a book on Marcus Aurelius, a book left over from my daughter's high school Latin class. I opened the book and flipped through the pages, only to be brought to the lines that seemed to have been written for me: *If you are distressed by anything external, the pain is not due to the thing itself, but to your estimate of it; and this you have the power to revoke at any moment.* The serendipity was validation that when the student is ready the teacher will appear. Marcus Aurelius had been patiently waiting almost two thousand years to speak to me, and the basket beside my coffee table had patiently held his message until I was ready to receive it. I took those words to heart. Standing up to open a bottle of wine, I decided to forgo checking the door once again to make sure it was locked and instead took a deep breath, exhaling the tension and anxiety that had stored up in me during the day, especially everything related to the storm that had not yet materialized. When those thoughts had exited I locked them out, at least for the night.

I continue to practice yoga every day, both on and off the yoga mat. My on-the-mat practice consists mainly of restorative yoga and yoga *nidra*-both of which activate the parasympathetic nervous system. In layman's terms, they help me to de-stress and relax. I practice restorative yoga to rest my mind and body. The practice uses a lot of props like soft blocks, bolsters, and blankets to support the body as we hold the yoga poses for as long as 15 minutes. The *nidra* in yoga *nidra* means sleep in Sanskrit. The purpose of yoga *nidra* is to relax the body and mind until one appears to be in a sleeplike state. But it's a dynamic state in which the subconscious mind is activated. I use the on-the-mat practices to calm down and connect with my subconscious. I feel so relaxed and refreshed after the practices, totally ready to look with new eyes on my life. To be completely transparent, I've fallen asleep more than once in my yoga *nidra* class, awakened by the sound

Serendipity

of my own snoring. Not my proudest moment, but still a fine practice.

Off the mat I try to live in the present. This was, and continues to be, a real challenge: to let go and just *be*. It is a challenge to trust that all I need will be provided and that the Universe (or God, or the Divine) holds for me a constant and unwavering love that is abundant and nonjudgmental. I have also begun to "go slow." When I read, I read. When I eat, I eat. I dropped multitasking as one of my skills, realizing that I can't focus on more than one thing at a time. I unplug more often, refusing to fill every waking moment with noise, sound, music, or the television. I turn things off in order to tune into my own spirit and what God has to say to me. I've learned to say no in a myriad of ways-without feeling guilty. I've grown to see that valuing my time means valuing myself.

I notice nature more: the pattern of fallen leaves on the driveway, the pinkish-orange color of the morning sky, the yellow sliver of the crescent moon against the dark of night, the songs of the birds that filter through an open window. I try to make Sunday a day of rest, when no errands are planned, where I give myself permission to do things that nourish me, like visiting family or friends, reading, or sitting on the porch listening to the wind chimes hanging in the tree. I create time each day for daydreaming, for I've found that I receive my greatest inspirations in those pauses where I stop thinking and become a channel to receive inspiration from God. And I've begun meditating, or stilling myself through silence, every day, if only for ten minutes. I've made gratitude part of my practice, all day, every day, and wake up giving thanks as my feet touch the floor. I keep a gratitude stone next to my bed to remind me each evening to name three things for which I am grateful before I close my eyes.

I've found it challenging to unlearn behaviors that I've practiced for over half a century. Recently, on a short trip from the library to the post office, I fell off the "living in the present/don't worry" wagon, and fell into a panic about student loans. *You do the math, Anne,* my evil twin whispered in my ear. *Who are you fooling, with this new way of living?*

I listened, pushed her aside, and thought a moment about what she had said, knowing that she wanted to bring me back to the dark side. And I was going to have none of it. *Move forward, Anne,* I countered. *Trust the process. All is well* became my walking mantra as I approached the post office. It continues to be my mantra whenever I can feel the negative thoughts bubbling up. My worried thoughts constrict me, strangle me.

Despite its challenges, this new way of living is always accompanied by benefits like peace and joy.

Serendipity

I lapse, sometimes greatly, especially around guilt, but the lapses are growing farther apart. And then I start again. I still worry, mostly about money and the health and safety of my children, mostly at night when I turn off the lights, the physical darkness calling to mind the perceived absence of light. But I'm soon reminded that the light never really goes away. And then the fear leaves, at least temporarily. It's going to take time for it to completely go away. Yoga has been instrumental in helping me to open my heart and to live in faith that there is an abundance of love available to me from God. What began as an evening of exercise on a hard floor under harsh lighting revealed a path. My purple yoga mat has become my magic carpet now, one brings me back to me and also helps me re-connect to God.

Namaste.

<u>Souvenirs:</u>

A new yoga mat and new yoga pants.

CHAPTER 10
PILGRIMAGE

*You cannot travel the path until
you have become the path itself.*

The Buddha

The pilgrimage sites described in this book are power places from which I draw inspiration. That which inspires us most certainly brings us to life. In fact, the Latin root for the word inspiration is *inspirationem,* which means "to breathe on" or "to breathe life into." Each pilgrimage was a spiritual resuscitation, a jump start to my failing faith. I found tranquility, peace of mind, and a heart-opening with the pilgrimages. At each site I would get inklings that encouraged me to look deeper within myself to find what I was seeking in life-be it happiness, security, love, or harmony. These nudges were life-affirming in a quiet way, so quiet that I had to still myself to hear the soft whisperings of my soul. I was beginning to experience first-hand what the mystics, saints, Jesus, and the Buddha all said: quiet yourself to know yourself.

The pilgrimages were horizontal, moving over space and time. They were also simultaneously vertical, directing me upward to the heavens. Each site was rooted in the physical, but I soon came to experience what was so eloquently described by Richard Rohr, "The visible world is an active doorway to the invisible world, and the invisible world is much larger than the visible." Some of the locations, like Glastonbury, are renowned sites where people have been making pilgrimages for over thousands of years. These are the places where some believe the veil between the seen and unseen worlds is very thin and penetrable. Other sites, like my yoga mat, were much more personal power places. But at each I received positive, supportive energy. Each pilgrimage supported the belief I have come to embrace, that unless I infuse my life with the insights gained through the experiences, the trips would be reduced to merely discrete experiences. While each place might have moved me deeply and provided lasting impressions, unless I used it to open myself to God, especially that which resides within *me*, the pilgrimages would be relegated to vacation memories, the sole justification to continue buying my monthly yoga pass, or taking the occasional drive to Philadelphia. The words of Ravi Raindra resonated, "Each place is the right place. The place where I am now can be a sacred space."

Initially I viewed travel as selfish, a time with no obligations, no expectations but now I view it as self-preservation. This unscheduled time allows for the possibility of spontaneity, exploration. Travel by its very nature expands: it pushes boundaries. It encouraged me to widen my view and my definition of myself.

I have a tendency to over-pack when I travel. On my first trip to England I took a small suitcase just for shoes because, well, you never know what you'll need. But I realized that I was also carrying around a lot of emotional baggage as well. Heavy baggage does not make for light travel. Over time I learned how to "pack" differently-trusting that I would have just the right clothes (and shoes) that I needed and if not, oh well, I'd make do. I also learned to leave behind the baggage of guilt for being "self-indulgent."

The French author Marcel Proust wrote, "The true journey of discovery consists not in seeking new landscapes, but in having fresh eyes." The pilgrimages caused me to look at how much of my true self I was allowing to show up in my life; the true self that by its very nature is calm, peaceful, secure, loving, generous, and certain. The opposite of the true self is the ego that operates out of emotions such as lack, fear, uncertainly, anger, and total self-absorption. I questioned whether I was planting seeds of myself in the world through my words, actions, and thoughts and whether I was showing up authentically in all of my relationships. I wondered whether I would depart this body having spent myself: that is, having given myself in service to those with whom I shared my time on the Earth. Or would I depart having been totally absorbed in the ego state as so beautifully articulated by George Harrison in his song *I, Me, Mine*? This same sentiment can also found in the Hindu scripture, the *Bahgavad Gita*, which reads: "They are forever free who...break away from the ego-cage of "I," "Me," "Mine" to be united with the Lord. That is the supreme state."

It was sobering to realize that for decades I had been holding back my true self out of fear of moving from my comfort zone, which in honesty was a totally uncomfortable place to be. I looked at how many times I acted out of a feeling of lack, or from wanting to play small, even though intuitively I knew better. My ego was driving me to a life of martyrdom-doing everything for everyone-and victimhood-the "poor me" syndrome. I discovered that the more I showed up in my own life in an authentic way-doing what brought me joy, using my gifts such as teaching and writing-the more I received in terms of opportunities to use these gifts, and the more I was also able to give in a healthy, balanced way.

Once I had begun, it was important to continue the pilgrimages in mind and heart, walking with the Divine. The pilgrimages helped me find parts of me that had separated from my soul, the parts of me that had spent decades wandering through different relationships, situations, and even physical locations searching for what would bring me the joy I felt was lacking in my life. The pilgrimages served as a beacon in the dark for finding those lost parts of me. They changed how I viewed and valued myself and ultimately were the catalysts that led to what I now understand was the reunion with my soul. I took the first steps to honoring myself and that included speaking more kindly to myself, learning to say no to things that drained me and, here's the big one-believing that I deserved to be joyful.

While on the pilgrimages I felt what it was like to live connected to my soul, to experience what Kahlil Gibran wrote: "Say not, I have found the one true path of Spirit. Say, rather, I have

Serendipity

wonderfully met the Spirit walking on my path." To extend this feeling into my daily existence, I continue to work to reposition myself at the center of my life, undoing decades of behaviors that pushed me to the fringes of my own life that had me living a depleting life of self-imposed *servitude* instead of a much different, healthier, and nourishing life of *service*.

I began the book writing about the pilgrimage route called the Camino. After completing the Camino, some pilgrims continue on to Cape Finisterre in Spain as their final stop. Known since ancient times as "the end of the earth," the pilgrims traditionally leave behind what they no longer need to carry on their journey such as clothes and boots. Some go a bit further and burn the items. The journey we are all on does not end at the sea, at land's end. The sea is not the end of the earth; it's the end of firm ground under our feet. The next step is to wade into the water, into fluidity, to go with the flow. It's a step into the unknown, another part of travel. It's a willingness to lose our footing to regain the ability to hear the voice of our soul. A poem by Rainer Maria Rilke titled "The Swan" (and translated into English by Robert Bly) beautifully summarizes this next step in which the swan leaves the hard ground and lowers itself into the flowing water.

The swan, unmoving and marvelously calm,
Is pleased to be carried, each moment more fully
*   grown,*
More like a king, further and further on.

Ultimately, all pilgrimages end up back home; I was led back to my home within. I encourage you to look back on your life and remember those places of pilgrimage, those places of power, that brought you home to your true self.

ACKNOWLEDGEMENTS

It took many years and the support of many friends and family to write this book. Some of them you've met on the pages of this book, others are behind-the-scenes cheerleaders - all of them are loved and appreciated.

Thanks to Marlee LeDai and Darla Bruno for their editing skills, and Jota Dazza at Bat Cat Creative for the book cover design. For the curious, the front cover photo was taken by me at Monk Bretton Priory in England, the back cover photo was taken by my daughter, Emily Rose in Rome.

Thanks to Amy Oscar, Sarah Bamford Seidelmann, and Jennifer Criswell for reviewing the book.

Thank you to Patty Robinson for driving with me on those rural South Jersey roads as we chased our dreams and for scoring us those tickets to the Mike Douglas Show.

Love to my in-laws, Rosemary and David Pells, who welcomed my daughters and me into their Yorkshire family.

To the generations of family members who I write about in this book - although we never met in person, your courage and love of family endure.

To David Wright, the road may not have always been smooth but a lot of the path was bathed in sunlight.

Love to my aunts Lisa Ciampoli and Tiny McCormick, my respective Godmothers for Confirmation and Baptism, to my uncles, Guy Ciampoli, Denny McCormick, and George Clarke, and to my aunt Mary Clarke whose own book on our family spurred my interest in researching my ancestry.

Love to Tommy Ciampoli and Regina Kuhn who have been my best friends for as long as I can remember.

Love to my grandparents, Al and Rose Aita and Anne and Joe Greco - the values you instilled in me continue to guide me every day.

Love to my sister and my brother-in-law, Rosemarie and Chuck Butler. Thanks for reading the manuscript in all its stages and for always opening your shore home to me - you probably don't know that I wrote some of the book while sitting on the deck.

Love to my brother, Joe, sister-in-law, Kim, and nephews, Joey and Michael Greco who round out our crazy Italian-American family.

Serendipity

Love and thanks to my parents, Annette and Joe Greco, for being my greatest cheerleaders. Your love and inspiration have been the foundation upon which I've built my life. Thank you for infusing my world with the music of Frank Sinatra and for teaching me the importance of family, laughter, and a dry sense of humor.

Love and thanks to my husband, Martin Pells, for reading the many drafts of this book, for indulging my love of British Invasion music, and for driving me to Liverpool every time we visit England.

Finally, love and thanks to my daughters, Alanna Kali and Emily Rose. You are my greatest teachers. I'm so grateful you chose me. You are my world.

CPSIA information can be obtained
at www.ICGtesting.com
Printed in the USA
BVHW041957200222
629604BV00015B/1111

9 780692 903605